SHEPHERD'S NOTES
Christian Classics

Spurgeon's Lectures to My Students

BROADMAN
&HOLMAN
PUBLISHERS

Nashville, Tennessee

Shepherd's Notes—Spurgeon's *Lectures to My Students*
© 1998
by Broadman & Holman Publishers
Nashville, Tennessee
All rights reserved
Printed in the United States of America

0-8054-9196-1
Dewey Decimal Classification: 251
Subject Heading: SPURGEON
Library of Congress Card Catalog Number: 98-21294

Library of Congress Cataloging-in-Publication Data

Meredith, Albert, 1946–
Charles Haddon Spurgeon's Lectures to my students / Albert Meredith, editor [i.e. author].
     p. cm.   — (Shepherd's notes. Christian classics)
     Includes bibliographical references.
     ISBN 0-8054-9196-1
     1. Spurgeon, C. H. (Charles Haddon), 1834–1892. Lectures to my students. 2. Preaching. I. Title. II. Series.
     BV4211.S68943M47   1998
     251—dc21

                             98-21294
                              CIP

1 2 3 4 5 6   03 02 01 00 99 98

Contents

Dear Reader:

Shepherd's Notes—Classics Series is designed to give you a quick, step-by-step overview of some of the enduring treasures of the Christian faith. They are designed to be used alongside the classic itself—either in individual study or in a study group.

Classics have staying power. Although they were written in a particular place and time and often in response to situations different than our own, they deal with problems, concerns, and themes that transcend time and place.

The faithful of all generations have found spiritual nourishment in the Scriptures and in the works of Christians from earlier generations. Martin Luther and John Calvin would not have become who they were apart from their reading Augustine. God used the writings of Martin Luther to move John Wesley from a religion of dead works to an experience at Aldersgate in which his "heart was strangely warmed."

It is an awesome sight—these streams of gracious influence flowing from generation to generation.

Shepherd's Notes—Classics Series will help you take the first steps in claiming and drawing strength from your spiritual heritage.

Shepherd's Notes is designed to bridge the gap between now and then and to help you understand, love, and benefit from the company of saints of an earlier time. Each volume gives you an overview of the main themes dealt with by the author and then walks with you step-by-step through the classic.

Enjoy!
In Him,

David R. Shepherd
Editor-in-Chief

DESIGNED FOR THE BUSY USER'

Shepherd's Notes for Spurgeon's *Lectures to My Students* is designed to provide an easy-to-use tool for gaining a quick overview of the major themes and the structure of Spurgeon's *Lectures*.

Shepherd's Notes are designed for laymen, pastors, teachers, small-group leaders and participants, as well as the classroom student.

DESIGNED FOR QUICK ACCESS

Persons with time restraints will especially appreciate the timesaving features built into *Shepherd's Notes*. All features are designed to work together to aid a quick and profitable encounter with *Lectures*—to point the reader to sections in *Lectures* where they may want to spend more time and go deeper.

Book-at-a-Glance. Provides a listing of the major sections of the *Lectures*.

Summary. Each of the lectures is summarized section by section.

Shepherd's Notes—Commentary. Following the summary of the lecture, a commentary is provided. This enables the reader to look back and see the major themes that make up that particular lecture.

Icons. Various icons in the margin provide information to help the reader better understand that part of the text. Icons include:

Shepherd's Notes Icon. This icon denotes the commentary section of each book of the *Lectures*.

Scripture Icon. Scripture verses often illuminate passages in *Lectures*.

Historical Background Icon. Many passages in *Lectures* are better understood in the light of historical, cultural, biographical, and geographical information.

Quotes Icon. This icon marks significant quotes from *Lectures.*

Points to Ponder Icon. These questions and suggestions for further thought will be especially useful in helping both individuals and groups see the relevance of *Lectures* for our time.

INTRODUCTION

Charles Haddon Spurgeon was known as the "Prince of Preachers" in an age when Great Britain had many legendary preachers. The twentieth century looks to the realm of sports, cinema, and music for its superstars; but the Victorians idolized their religious leaders. London street-sellers sold cheap statuettes of popular preachers, and none were more popular than those of Spurgeon.

Spurgeon regularly spoke to crowds of five and six thousand without the aid of microphones. During the thirty-seven years of his ministry in London (1854–1891), over fourteen thousand members were added to the congregation he pastored.

Spurgeon was one of the most widely read authors of the century. During his lifetime, his sermons were published each week. Even after his death in 1892, his publishers continued for another quarter century printing sermons that had not been published. Some have estimated that over 100 million copies were sold in his lifetime alone, and many are being reprinted in our generation.

The *Pall Mall Gazette* described Spurgeon as "the most popular English author of the day" in 1883. This was in an age that included Charles Dickens, George Elliot and Robert Louis Stevenson.

In addition to his printed sermons, Spurgeon also published a number of other works such as *John Plowman's Talk* and *John Plowman's Pictures*, common tales on everyday life, and *The Treasury of David*, a monumental commentary on the Psalms.

Spurgeon's *Lectures to My Students*—perhaps his most important and lasting work—is filled with practical advice from the "Prince of Preachers" and remains a classic on pastoral ministry. It arose out of his weekly lectures to the students at the Pastor's College, which he began soon after he started his ministry in London. Spurgeon felt the college was his "first-born and most beloved" work. What began as a mentoring program soon grew to a full-fledged training school for pastors. It lives on today as Spurgeon's College, still training people for ministry.

HISTORICAL SETTING

The nineteenth century was an age of progress in Western Europe, especially England. The growing development of human society was the predominant theme of popular literature. Darwin's *Origin of Species* explained how nature progressed; Marx's *Das Capital* told how history was unfolding. Eventually Sigmund Freud sought to explain how the human psyche had developed.

The nineteenth century produced more "utopias" than all the rest of western literature combined.

The fruits of the Industrial Revolution were being passed down to the common people. The right to vote was being expanded, first to the middle class, and then to the working class. Scientific discoveries extended life expectancy and improved living conditions.

The nineteenth century was also an age of relative peace. From Waterloo in 1815 to the outbreak of World War I in 1914, Europe enjoyed a period of general tranquillity. Most wars were on the fringes of civilization. There were even suggestions that war might be a thing of the past.

But the century was also a time of serious premonitions. The Victorians appeared to be rooted in dogmatic confidence; but some were beginning to raise serious doubts. If evolution is true, can the Bible be trusted? If history is merely the development of class warfare, where does God fit in? From the European Continent came "higher criticism" of the Bible which severely questioned the authenticity and accuracy of Scripture. Ancient dogmas were being called into question.

Spurgeon was caught up in these issues. From the 1870s onward, he took seriously the growth of theological liberalism and became one of the primary champions for the cause of the historic Christian faith. He feared the church was on the verge of another theological Dark Age. In the earlier part of his career he had been one of the central figures in a general movement to soften the differences between Protestants, but the last years of his life were spent in a discouraging campaign known as the "Downgrade Controversy."

Spurgeon publicly expressed his concern about the inroads of liberalism into the Baptist Union of England and pled for a return to orthodoxy. When asked to give specific names and cases to his general charges, Spurgeon refused because he had promised his sources he would not. The division widened and led to his break with the Baptist Union. Not long afterward Spurgeon died.

BIOGRAPHICAL SECTION

Roots

Charles Haddon Spurgeon was born on June 19, 1834, in the village of Kelvedon, Essex, the first son of John and Eliza Spurgeon. His ancestry has been traced to the Dutch Calvinists who came to England in the sixteenth century and included many preachers; one was imprisoned during the Restoration Period.

Childhood

Spurgeon's father was a coal merchant and a lay preacher at a small Independent (Congregational) chapel. Much of Charles' early life was spent growing up in the home of his grandfather

John Bunyan (1628–1688) wrote *Pilgrim's Progress*, second only to the Bible itself in total sales, and *Grace Abounding to the Chief of Sinners*. Perhaps no one was more influential upon Spurgeon's thought and life.

At the time of his death, there were over twelve thousand volumes in Spurgeon's personal library. Over half of these are preserved at William Jewell College in Liberty, Missouri.

who was also an Independent minister. A precocious child, he loved reading the Puritans (especially Bunyan) and memorizing hymns. The only make-believe game he would play was gathering the neighborhood children and delivering the "sermon" as they played "church."

As a young student, he remained at the top of his class—with one brief exception. For some strange reason, his grades fell one cold winter; and he was sent to the foot of the class. His teacher was befuddled until he realized the last row was closest to the stove. He rearranged the seating and young Spurgeon's grades once again soared.

Although Spurgeon never attended college, he was far from uneducated. His childhood education surpassed that of most of his contemporaries; and his precocity left him with an abiding curiosity which went far beyond the classroom. Throughout his life he was a voracious reader and student—not only of theology, but also of history, literature, science, and other subjects.

Early Career

Spurgeon was converted at fifteen in a Primitive Methodist chapel and he began to preach regularly in the village of Waterbeach, six miles from Cambridge, at the age of seventeen. From the start, soul winning was the main thrust of his ministry. This evangelistic passion remained with him throughout his career. While he was concerned with sound doctrine, social ministries, educational and political issues, all of these were secondary to his desire to reach the unbeliever.

In just a few months' time, the tiny congregation at Waterbeach grew to over four hundred members. Many who came to hear the "boy wonder" speak were skeptical and cautious but were soon won over by the depth of his message and the earnestness of his spirit, as well as his oratorical skills.

After two years at Waterbeach, he received a call to preach at the historic New Park Street Chapel in London. Although the church had been without a pastor for several years and had fallen on hard times, Spurgeon was convinced there was some mistake when he received the invitation. There was no mistake.

London Ministry

Approximately 120 or so attended that morning in December of 1854; but when Spurgeon returned for the evening service, the crowd had more than doubled. They soon called this Essex youth to be their pastor, and neither the church nor the city was ever the same.

Within a matter of months the sanctuary, which seated 1,200, was filled to overflowing. Before a year had passed the congregation was forced to enlarge the auditorium. While the renovation took place, they met in downtown London at Exeter Hall, which seated over 4,500 and was the site of the annual meeting of various Christian societies. From the first, crowds had to be turned away at the door. This news led to even larger crowds.

During his thirty-seven years of ministry in London, fourteen thousand new converts were added to the rolls of his church. He did not give an "altar call," *per se*, but seekers were received for counseling and instruction, usually on Tuesday evenings at the church.

Not everyone was pleased at the popularity of the young preacher from Essex. Even within the church, people complained about his lack of formal education and the plainness and passion of his speech. One fellow pastor even went on record as doubting his conversion! The complaints and accusations only served to swell the crowds even more; and Spurgeon just kept on preaching—twice on Sunday and several times throughout the week.

In 1856, the church took the unprecedented step of renting the Surrey Music Hall, a location in south London, for their evening services. Many were shocked at the use of a secular auditorium for religious purposes. Others thought it presumptuous, to say the least, considering the hall seated over twelve thousand. The newspapers were filled with letters and editorials on the subject as the time drew near.

On October 19, 1856, the hall was filled completely with thousands still outside. Every vacant spot was taken by the curious, the pious, and the critical. As Spurgeon began to preach, someone—it has never been determined who—shouted, "Fire!" A panic-stricken stampede began. Men and women leaped from the balcony as the congregation became a mob. Spurgeon himself fainted and was carried out of the building. Seven died and scores were seriously injured. Spurgeon suffered what might be diagnosed today as a nervous breakdown and remained secluded in recovery for over a month. The services at the Surrey Music Hall were changed to Sunday morning in the hopes that the crowd would be less volatile.

Only Wesley and Whitefield of the eighteenth century, preaching in the open air without the aid of microphones, compare to this. Little wonder Whitefield suffered with a bleeding larynx.

The criticism that followed only served to heighten interest in this young preacher. Hardly a place could be found large enough to hold the crowds. Services at the Surrey Music Hall continued for over three years where over fifteen thousand regularly attended. The largest crowd Spurgeon ever spoke to was 23,654 at the Crystal Palace on a national day of mourning after the Indian Mutiny of 1857.

Meanwhile Spurgeon's congregation was building on the south side of London an edifice they hoped would be worthy of their pastor's popularity. In 1861, they moved into the Metropolitan Tabernacle which seated nearly six thousand people. Spurgeon himself paid much of the cost of this building from speaking fees and from profits generated by his books and lectures. Preaching eight or ten times a week, in addition to giving various lectures, was not uncommon for him.

The strain of his exhausting schedule and the pressure of knowing that every word was being transcribed for publication eventually took its toll. Spurgeon soon found himself dealing with bouts of deep depression. Melancholy produced by the stress of his work, plus the unrelenting pain of gout, required yearly visits to the south of France where his soul and body could be refreshed by the warm, coastal sunshine and breezes of the Mediterranean Sea.

Spurgeon's home life was necessarily quiet and tranquil. Soon after coming to London, he met, courted, and married Susannah Thompson. She gave birth to twin sons in 1856, both of whom eventually entered the ministry. Although Susannah Spurgeon was a semi-invalid, she made their home a much-needed haven for Spurgeon and also helped in his ministry, especially distributing good literature to the poor.

Charles Haddon Spurgeon was both a visionary and a child of his age. He was considered a radical by many for his refusal to wear the traditional frock coat of nonconformists. He disdained the Latinized speech which had become customary in the pulpit of his day. Instead, he spoke in earthy Saxon terms and spiced his sermons with illustrations and humor. In order to reach his generation, Spurgeon took the church to the people, preaching

The five characteristics that summarize Spurgeon's ministry are:

1. Earnestness— He said this was "the most essential quality for successful ministry."
2. Simplicity— He refused ordination and the title of "Reverend."
3. Industriousness— He worked 16–18 hours each day, dictating to one secretary after another.
4. Practicality— He was no mystic, but sought to relate faith to everyday matters.
5. Zest for life— The humor in his sermons is still obvious today.

wherever the crowds would gather. His Tabernacle was the forerunner of the modern mega-churches of the late twentieth century.

Spurgeon, however, remained Victorian to the core in his approach to social problems and his optimistic beliefs in progress. He refused to modify his preaching to reflect the changes that Darwinism and historical criticism were bringing. His obituary in *The Daily Chronicle* read: "Mr. Spurgeon remained an eloquent voice crying in the wilderness, and preaching the old notions with the old face and in the old intensity of personal belief" (*The Daily Chronicle*, February 1, 1892).

Impact of Lectures to My Students

Spurgeon considered his Pastor's College his most important work. Through his students he multiplied his ministry, training hundreds of pastors who preached throughout the world. Spurgeon's College is still the largest Baptist theological school in Europe today.

The lectures were imminently practical, dealing with such issues as choosing a text, developing one's voice, using and finding illustrations, posture, gestures; the practice of public and private prayer; as well as handling personal depression.

Spurgeon was more than a wonder in his own day. Each surviving generation seems to rediscover him anew. "Tell all that you know . . . and buy Spurgeon!" wrote Helmut Thielicke in his *Encounter with Spurgeon*.

Warren Weirsbe in his *Walking with the Giants* said, "Above all else, read Spurgeon himself! Get a *complete* edition of *Lectures to My Students* and read it carefully. . . . 'The Minister's Fainting Fits' and 'The Need of Decision for the

Chronology of Spurgeon's Life

DATE	EVENT
1834	Born at Kelvedon, Essex, on June 19
1834–40	Lived with his grandparents in Stambourne
1840	Returned to his parents' home in Colchester
1850	Converted in Primitive Methodist Chapel, in Colchester, in January
1850	Baptized at Isleham, May 3, in the River Lark
1850	Attended Mr. Luding's school in Cambridge, in August
1851	Became the pastor of Waterbeach Baptist Church
1854	Became the pastor of New Park Street Chapel in London, in April
1855	Began to preach at Exeter Hall on the Strand while renovations were made at New Park Street Chapel, in February
1855	T. W. Medhurst became Spurgeon's first ministerial student. This led eventually to the Pastor's College, in July.
1856	Married Susannah Thompson on January 8
1856	Twin sons, Thomas and Charles, were born on September 20.
1857	Preached to 23,654 people at the Crystal Palace at a national response to the Indian Rebellion, on October 7
1861	Services begin in the Metropolitan Tabernacle on March 18.
1862	Famous "Baptismal Regeneration" sermon that sparked a controversy with the Church of England began on June 5
1866	Colportage Association founded
1867	Stockwell Orphanage for boys founded
1879	Stockwell Orphanage for girls founded
1880	Moved his home from Clapham to Norwood
1887	First "Down Grade" article appeared in *The Sword and Trowel* in August, igniting the controversy within the Baptist Union.
1891	Last sermon preached at the Metropolitan Tabernacle, on June 7
1892	Died on January 31

Truth' ought to be required reading for all ministerial students."

Introduction and Apology
"These addresses were not originally prepared for the public eye."

Each lecture was given at the end of a long week of study when the students were "weary with sterner studies." So, Spurgeon spoke on practical issues, but in a lively, often humorous and personal manner.

The lectures were not originally intended for publication, and Spurgeon defended all his personal allusions as those of a father telling his son his own life story—the story of an old soldier explaining how battles were fought.

Spurgeon also explained that the lectures were intended for practical purposes.

Purpose of the Lectures

"The age has become intensely practical, and needs a ministry not only orthodox and spiritual, but also natural in utterance and practically shrewd. . . .It's delicious to put one's foot through the lath and plaster of old affections, to make room for the granite walls of reality."

 **COMMENTARY**

Spurgeon was both a traditionalist and an iconoclast. As a traditionalist, his message was rooted in the doctrine of grace of the Puritans, Calvin, and Augustine. He adamantly opposed the liberalism of modern theology.

On the other hand, Spurgeon's practicality led him to break with outdated traditions. His preaching style resonated with the common man. He spoke plainly, humorously, and directly to the heart. He dressed simply. He refused to be ordained, not willing to let them "lay their empty hands on his empty head."

These lectures, more than any other of Spurgeon's writings, reveal the essence of his public ministry and his personal convictions.

Lecture I—The Minister's Self-Watch

"Take heed to thyself, and unto the doctrine" (1 Tim. 4:16, KJV).

BOOK-AT-A-GLANCE

In this lecture Spurgeon emphasized the need for the minister to (1) be sure of his personal relationship with Christ, (2) look after his own spiritual growth, and (3) cultivate his own personal character.

SUMMARY:

Just as Michelangelo understood the importance of his tools and always insisted on making his own brushes with his own hands, the minister must take personal care of his own body, soul and spirit.

"It is not great talent God blesses so much as likeness to Jesus. A holy minister is an awful weapon in the hand of God."—Robert Murray McCheyne (1813–1843)

Preaching, which Spurgeon believed to be the primary task of the minister, involves his voice, his intellect, and his spirit. Involving the spirit is the most important.

John Bunyan is perhaps the only person Spurgeon quoted more often than McCheyne. Considered by many to be the most Christ-like man Scotland ever produced, McCheyne saw revival come to the Church of Scotland, although he only lived 29 years.

It should be one of our first cares that we ourselves be saved men.

"Whatever 'call' a man may pretend to have, if he has not been called to holiness, he certainly has not been called to the ministry."

Unconverted preachers are:

- Unhappy—Their pulpits are to them what an oar is to a galley slave.

The Puritan, Richard Baxter, in his classic work, *The Reformed Pastor*, also advised his fellow-pastors that they should principally and repeatedly take heed that they were saved men. John Bunyan in his treatise, "Sighs from Hell," also warned of 'blind priests' who have been the means of leading many souls to destruction.

- Unserviceable—like one who comes across folks dying of thirst and has no water to give.
- Mischievous—delaying the unregenerate in to thinking they are right with God. An unsaved pastor is sure eventually to reveal character flaws.

It is of the next importance to the minister that his piety be vigorous.

Pastors are "the choicest of his [God's] choice, the elect of his election."

Pastors are to possess the highest moral character because:

- Others take their cue spiritually from the pastor.
- The minister is subject to great temptations.
- The difficulty of the task requires character.

The minister should take care that his personal character agrees in all respects to his ministry.

Both sound doctrine and a fruitful life are needed.

The scrutiny of a watching world should extend to little things such as small debts, unpunctuality, gossip, petty quarrels, coarseness or discourteousness, and our recreations.

COMMENTARY

Spurgeon seemed to believe that open immorality disqualified him from pastoral ministry and was "a fatal" sign that ministerial graces were never in the man's character.

In recent years, the church has witnessed the regrettable fall of a number of high-profile clergy. Some, however, have been successfully restored to ministry. The moral failures of society in general are finding their way into the parsonage with increasing persistency. One poll determined that twelve percent of its evangelistic leaders had engaged in sexually inappropriate behavior. Whether they can be fully restored to ministry is still a question.

Spurgeon summarized the work of the ministry: "To face the enemies of truth, to defend the bulwark of faith, to rule well in the house of God, to comfort all that mourn, to edify the saint, to guide the perplexed, to bear with the forward, to win and nurse souls."

LECTURE II—THE CALL TO THE MINISTRY

"That hundreds have missed their way and stumbled against a pulpit is sorrowfully evident from the fruitless ministries and decaying churches which surround us."

Spurgeon affirmed that while all believers are called to communicate the gospel, there is a special calling for those who teach and "bear rule" in the church and are supported by the church. He suggested some "signs" of God's special calling:

- An intense, all absorbing desire for the work. "Do not enter the ministry if you can help it."
- An aptitude to teach. Other important attributes include sound judgment, solid experience, gentle manners, a loving spirit, firmness and courage, tenderness and sympathy.
- The fruit of evangelism.

"Brethren, if the Lord gives you no zeal for souls, keep to the lapstone or the trowel, but avoid the pulpit."

- The call from the local church. Though not an infallible sign of God's will, the request of a local congregation for your ministry is a necessary ingredient.

Spurgeon often found it necessary to judge the reality of ministerial call of applicants to the Pastor's College. Reasons he felt they were not called were: (1) overambition to shine among men; (2) lack of sufficient intelligence; (3) lack of endurance or experience; (4) zealousness without substance; (5) aspiring to the ministry for lack of any direction; (6) physical deficiencies such as a speech impediment; (7) instability of theological convictions; and (8) ability to weather the storms of the ministry with grace.

It is to God's glory that He uses all kinds of people and revels in blessing the most unlikely in a greater way.

 COMMENTARY

Spurgeon insisted that the gift of prophecy and the office of pastor are part of God's special calling to ministries. However, we might seriously question whether the gift of prophecy belongs to pastoral ministry. Whether it is the "forth-telling" of God's specific will for the body or merely bold proclamation of truth, we see in both Scripture and church people who were not pastors who had the gift, and successful pastors who did not.

Spurgeon also mentioned that the gift of evangelism is "a necessary part of God's call to the ministry." He said, "Surely it were better to be a muck-raker, or a chimney-sweep, than to stand in the ministry as an utterly barren tree."

This is certainly open to debate. Consider those faithful shepherds laboring in difficult places. Consider missionaries who have barely a handful of converts after a lifetime of faithful ministry. Would the need for the gift of evangelism have disqualified the prophet Jeremiah? Spurgeon, like so many of us, may have been guilty of "gifts projection"—the tendency to make the gifts and passions God has given us normative for the entire church. While every believer is called to witness to a lost world, only some have the God-given gift of harvesting. While all are called upon to be merciful, only some have the gift of mercy. While all are required to give to the work of the kingdom, only some are blessed with the gift of giving by which many are blessed.

Spurgeon also disqualified some on the basis of physical deficiencies, such as speech impediments—a dangerous practice. Did not Moses stutter? Did not the apostle Paul admit to lack of eloquence? Thomas Aquinas was so slow of speech he was thought to be mentally handicapped at first. Many pastors have been marvelously used by God in spite of lisping tongues and distracting physical handicaps.

LECTURE III—THE PREACHER'S PRIVATE PRAYER

"Of course the preacher is above all others distinguished as a man of prayer . . . . If you become lax in secret devotion, not only will you need to be pitied, but your people also."

Spurgeon emphasized the critical necessity of prayer in the ministry. When asked the secret of his success as a pastor, he would most often reply, "My people pray for me."

"All our libraries and studies are mere emptiness compared with our closets. We grow, we wax mighty, we prevail in private prayer."

- The minister is to be in a continual *spirit* of prayer that goes beyond his regular time in the closet of prayer.
- Prayer is essential while preparing sermons. Texts of Scripture are often made clearer through prayer.
- Prayer is needed both prior to and during the act of preaching. The pastor who has been wrestling with God in prayer for his people is more apt to preach in earnest.

Spurgeon also felt that his "freshest and best thoughts" in the pulpit often had come as he prayed silently while he was preaching. One of the central factors of his pulpit ministry was his extemporaneous reading and running commentary upon the Scripture, which was separate from the sermon itself.

Theodorus on Luther: "I overheard him in prayer but, good God, with what life and spirit did he pray!"

- The minister should pray after the sermon either for comfort in disappointment or praise for blessings.
- The preacher must intercede daily for the needs of his congregation. Pray for the sick and the soul-sick; for the unsaved and the

seeking; for the depressed and the back-sliding; for the widow's tears and the orphan's sighs.

- Prayer is essential if a pastor is to have "unction" in his ministry. Spurgeon strongly recommends periodic prayer retreats alone or with two or three godly men for several days.

COMMENTARY

While Spurgeon's schedule often consisted of eighteen-hour days, each year he would withdraw to the south of France for four or five weeks of solitude, rest, and prayer. It was there that his soul was refreshed and his mind and body were restored. Virtually every great saint in church history has shared in the need for prolonged, concerted prayer.

Martin Luther—"I have so much business I cannot get on without spending three hours daily in prayer."

John Wesley—devoted two hours daily to intercession.

Adoniram Judson—withdrew seven times a day to pray in secret.

John Calvin—"Words fail to express how necessary prayer is. . . . While the Keeper of Israel neither slumbers nor sleeps, yet He is inactive, as if forgetting us, when He sees us idle and mute."

Thomas Hooker—"Prayer is my life work, and it is by means of it that I carry out the rest."

William Carey—"Prayer—secret, fervent, believing prayer—lies at the root of all personal godliness."

E. M. Bounds—"The character of our praying will determine the character of our preaching. Light praying makes light preaching."

William Cowper and John Newton—"Satan trembles when he sees the weakest sinner upon his knees."

Jack Hayford—"If we don't, He won't."

Jesus—"Men ought always to pray and not faint."

LECTURE IV—OUR PUBLIC PRAYER

Dissenters were the English churches who refused to follow the Church of England in terms of worship and polity. Originally called "Nonconformists" in the seventeenth century, they were the Presbyterians, Baptists, Independents (Congregationalists), and Methodists of England.

Popular opinion in Victorian England was that people attended liturgical churches to worship and pray, but Dissenters assembled mainly to hear sermons. While Spurgeon did not entirely agree with this, he did admit that regarding public prayer: "There is room for improvement, and in some quarters there is an imperative demand for it."

- Free prayer, as opposed to written liturgies, is the most scriptural. Nowhere in the Bible can one find prescribed prayer.

- Public prayer must be earnest, spiritual, and from the heart. While it was said of Jesus, "Never a man spoke like this," His disciples pleaded, "Lord, teach us to pray."

- Our public prayers must have a heavenly frame of mind. They must be solemn and humble—not flippant, loud, formal, or careless.

- The Lord must be the object of our prayers. Do not pray to impress men.

- Avoid all vulgarities in prayer. Avoid witticism or irreverence.
- Avoid the use of repetitive phrases. These are a distraction to the church body.
- Avoid appearing demanding of God. The boldness with which we approach the throne rises from grace and humility, not from an impertinent spirit.
- Pray when you pray, do not preach.
- When called upon to pray, conduct the prayer yourself. Never ask others to pray as a reward or recognition or out of a desire to give others something to do.
- Public prayers must come from the heart. Sleepy prayers will destroy a sermon before it starts.
- Public prayers must be appropriate. They need not chronicle the week's activities.
- Public prayer must not be too long. While you cannot pray too long in private, public prayers should be limited to no more than ten minutes.
- Do not use cant phrases. Spurgeon's day, like our own, was filled with religious phrases of questionable meaning and sincerity.
- Vary the order of service as much as possible in order to avoid dry ritualism.
- Vary the length of your prayers.
- Vary the subject of your prayers.
- Be genuine; be authentic.
- Prepare your public prayers. It is not so much the phraseology as it is the heart that needs preparation.

"If I may have my choice, I will sooner yield up the sermon than the prayer."

 ## COMMENTARY

When Spurgeon was called to New Park Street Church as a young man of nineteen, his first priority was to teach his people to pray. He loathed the petty, pious words and customary phrases that had become common in prayer. He prayed agonizingly, boldly, naturally, as a child to his father. Soon the prayers of the people began to reflect the earnestness of their pastor. Sometimes at their prayer meetings, the presence of God would be so real they would sit in awestruck silence.

Not all were favorably impressed, however, with Spurgeon's public prayers. The author, George Eliot (Mary Ann Evans), recorded her first impressions of Spurgeon:

Eliot was the author of *Silas Marner* and *Adam Bede* among other works. Religiously, she broke with orthodoxy and translated liberal writings from the Continent into English.

"It was the most superficial grocer's-back-parlour view of Calvinistic Christianity. . . . He said, 'Let us approach the throne of God,' very much as he might have invited you to take a chair."

Does Spurgeon's refusal to allow others to lead in public prayer conform to the concept of the priesthood of all Believers? Is the pastor the only one qualified to lead the congregation in prayer?

It is also interesting to note that the public prayers of the Puritans lasted forty-five minutes. Spurgeon suggests ten minutes. What is appropriate as the Church enters the twenty-first century at record speed?

LECTURE V—SERMONS— THEIR MATTER

"We cannot afford to utter pretty nothings. . . . Nothing can compensate for the absence of teaching."

- Sermons should have solid content in them about relevant truth. It is critical that the sermon be rooted in biblical theology. The preacher's crucial task is to dispense sound doctrine in his sermons.

- One's sermon must be congruous to the text. Spurgeon allowed for, and practiced, allegory and spiritualizing; but he insisted, "liberty must not degenerate into license."

- Sermons should be about certain profound and weighty content. There is no use in proclaiming truth that is patently obvious or irrelevant. Platitudinal verbiage will drown the congregation.

- Preach all the doctrines which constitute or lie around the gospel. Do not be afraid to preach deep theology, especially the truths of Calvinism. On the other hand, avoid the imbalance of preaching one truth to the neglect of others. Do not major on minors. Above all, center your preaching on Christ. So-called sermons that cast doubt about the authenticity of the text or the truth of Biblical accounts are the worst of all.

- Do not overload a sermon with too much matter. "You should make your sermon like a loaf of bread, fit for eating, and in convenient form."

- The matter should be well arranged. There should be a sense of sequential logic to it.

One response to the stentorian preaching of Spurgeon's day was that of the author, Robert Louis Stevenson (*Treasure Island, Dr. Jeckell and Mr. Hyde,* etc.), who wrote in his journal, "Went to church today. Was not greatly impressed."

21

"Preach Christ, always and evermore. He is the whole gospel. . . . If with the zeal of the Methodists we can preach the doctrine of the Puritans, a great future is before us."

- Doctrinal teaching should be clear. This necessitates the preacher be rooted in sound doctrine himself.
- Keep the content fresh. Avoid the "monotony of repetition."
- Continue to grow and develop. One's later sermons should have more depth and insight than the earlier ones.

 COMMENTARY

Although Spurgeon's oratorical skills were remarkable, far more of his sermons have been read than listened to. This indicates a depth of content independent of the delivery. A century later his sermons are still being published and sold. Many have referred to Spurgeon as "the Prince of Preachers." While his oratorical skills were unsurpassed in his day, it has been the content of his preaching that has caused his influence to linger with us today.

Three things might be said of the content of Spurgeon's sermons. First, Christ and the cross were the anchor of his theology. Second, Spurgeon aptly has been called "The Last of the Puritans" because he continued to hold to the doctrine of grace, which includes the total depravity of humankind, the election of the saints, and the sovereignty of God in all things.

Third, Spurgeon's preaching had both a familiar ring that captured the minds of the common people and the note of authority and conviction. He believed what he was preaching was true and relevant.

John Calvin—"None will ever be a good minister of the Word of God unless he is first of all a scholar."

Donald Grey Barnhouse—"If I had only three years to give to the Lord, I'd spend two years studying."

Alexander Whyte—"I would have all lazy ministers drummed out of the Assembly."

C. H. Spurgeon—"I have no belief in the ministry which ignores laborious preparation."

LECTURE VI—OF THE CHOICE OF A TEXT

Spurgeon gave earnest attention to every aspect of the worship service. Much prayer and attention should be given to the selection of a hymn and the reading of Scripture as well as the pastoral prayer.

If the preaching is to be rooted in the text, then the choosing of a text is critical.

- Do not be misled by the sound and apparent fitness of scriptural words. One unwise pastor preached the funeral of a troublesome deacon on the text, "It came to pass that the beggar died."
- Avoid a monotonous regularity. Pity the congregation whose pastor simply repeats his slender stock of sermons. He warned against resorting to the Lectionary of liturgical churches because doing so hinders the spontaneity of the Spirit.
- Choosing the text is a difficult task. The problem is not because texts are scarce, but because there are so many.
- Know the needs of your congregation. Consider the condition of their hearts, the

"I confess, I frequently sit hour after hour praying and waiting for a subject, and that this is the main part of my study."

sins with which they struggle, and the trials they are experiencing.

- Consider previous topics and seek for a balance. Doctrine, history, types, psalms, proverbs, experience, promise, invitation, rebuke or threatening—preach the whole of inspired truth.

Spurgeon was led to speak extemporaneously only on a few occasions. He usually spent every working moment in the shadow of the pulpit, gleaning information for future use.

COMMENTARY

Spurgeon disdained preaching sermon series. To him, doing so smacked of the flesh as opposed to the spontaneity of the Spirit. On the other hand, Dr. W. A. Criswell, for years the beloved pastor of First Baptist Church, Dallas, Texas, urges the use of sermon series to save the time and anguish Spurgeon describes in finding a text. Could not the Spirit inspire a series of sermons as well as a single one?

Homileticans have suggested that the preacher spend "one hour in the study for every minute in the pulpit." This would have been an impossibility for Spurgeon, who preached eight to ten times a week. Also, when might the modern pastor find this kind of time in a profession that demands more and more of leadership and expertise in areas not related to the pulpit?

To aid him in his research, Spurgeon had several researchers gleaning the resources of the British Museum. Few pastors today are blessed with such assistance. Nevertheless, we must agree that preachers are still called upon to preach, and preaching requires proper preparation. Above all, we are called upon to "feed the flock of God."

LECTURE VII—ON SPIRITUALIZING

"Within limit, my brethren, be not afraid to spiritualize."

Allegorizing or spiritualizing is finding in the text a hidden or implied truth not originally intended in a literal sense. Spurgeon begged to differ with those who spoke disparagingly of allegorical preaching. Yet he warned of overdoing it and gave sage advice.

- Do not strain the text by illegitimate spiritualizing. Do not twist the text to make it say what is not intended.
- Never spiritualize upon indelicate subjects. "Solomon's Song had better be let alone than dragged in the mire as it often is."
- Never spiritualize in order to parade your personal ingenuity.
- Do not allow your audience to forget that you are drawing spiritual truths from historical narratives that are, indeed, facts and not myths.
- Legitimate spiritualizing will include the various types found in the Old Testament, plenteous metaphors throughout Scripture, allegories that Scripture itself alludes to (i.e., Melchisedec in the book of Hebrews), universal principles of God's Word evidenced in the narrative, and the parables of Jesus which are, by nature, allegorical.

"Allegorical preaching debases the taste, and fetters the understanding of both preachers and hearers."—Adam Clarke

"Be sparing in allegorizing or spiritualizing."—John Wesley

SN COMMENTARY

Preaching from any text that goes beyond the doctrinal epistles of the New Testament will require some spiritualizing, if only to bring home the application. Every sermon demands a "What?" and a "So what?" without which it is only so much pedantic information. Laying out the practical truth of the text is where preachers most often go astray. As Spurgeon said, spiritualizing must be "guided by discretion and judgement."

Some preaching professors would have us avoid spiritualizing altogether, but doing so would break with the way of Scripture itself. How bereft of fire and illustrations the prophets would have been if they could not have used their gripping object lessons (Jeremiah's pottery, Zechariah's plumb line, Hosea's unfaithful wife). The apostle Paul's use of Abraham to illustrate the priority of faith, John's analogies of light and life, James' references to the tongue as a fire and a ship's rudder, not to mention the allegories that the writer of the book of Hebrews refers to repeatedly, all give evidence that Spirit-led allegorizing is a legitimate practice in discerning and proclaiming spiritual truth.

Lecture VIII— On the Voice

"The sweetest voice is nothing without something to say."

Spurgeon possessed one of the most commanding voices in the history of the church. He could be heard by every individual of the twenty thousand who came to the Crystal Palace. He offered the following rules about the voice.

- The first rule regarding the preachers' voice is, do not think too much about it. Content is more important than delivery.

- The second rule, however, is do not think too little about it. It is a travesty to speak of precious truth in a monotone.

- Avoid stentorian affectations when in the pulpit. Be natural; be genuine.

- Try to correct any disagreeable idiosyncrasies of speech that might distract from the message. Try to avoid local dialects, discordant squawks, nasal whines, or closing one's throat.

- Always speak so as to be heard. Volume must be accompanied by careful distinctness. Do not speak so slowly as to bore or frustrate your listener, or so rapidly as to make the message unintelligible.

- Generally, it is wise never to exert your voice to its limits. "Do not give your hearers head-aches when you mean to give them heart-aches."

- Vary the force of your voice. There are no rules about when to be soft or loud. Let the volume fit the point one is making. Never do anything merely for effect.

Spurgeon was called upon to preach the sermon on the National Day of Fasting over the Indian Rebellion on October 7, 1857. Officials counted 23,654 persons in the Crystal Palace pavilion on that occasion. Although he did not have the assistance of microphones or loud speakers, Spurgeon still could make himself heard.

Stentorian

Stentor was a Greek herald during Greece's war with Troy. He had a loud, commanding voice.

- Vary the tone of your voice as well as the volume.
- Always suit your voice to your matter. Above all, be natural in everything.
- Seek to develop your skills. Practice. Ask a friend to observe and offer constructive criticism.
- Take great care of your voice. Speak only when your throat is clear. Do not restrict it with clothing.

Spurgeon's oratorical skills were legendary. Mr. Sheridan Knowles, an actor, playwright, and teacher of elocution at Stepney College, directed his students to hear Spurgeon. "He is absolutely perfect in oratory. . . . He knows everything. He can do anything."

 COMMENTARY

Because Spurgeon's oratorical skill was natural rather than learned, he had little real help for those who struggled. The natural athlete seldom makes a good coach, because he does instinctively what others must accomplish only with studied practice. Call for variance in volume and tone is one thing, but when and how to vary them is the question.

Spurgeon claimed that hoarseness is often due to speaking too little—twice a week. He recommended preaching four to six times a week to strengthen the voice. Strangest of all his practices was keeping a glass of chilly vinegar and water on the pulpit to enliven his voice.

Dr. Jerry Vines, co–pastor of First Baptist Church of Jacksonville, Florida, gives much practical advise on caring for the preacher's throat in his book, *A Guide to Effective Sermon Delivery*. His main point is twofold: (1) the voice must be relaxed to perform properly, and (2) one's breathing must come from the abdomen.

The most pertinent of all advice in preaching is Spurgeon's plea, "Above all, in everything be natural." Do not imitate anyone, but be yourself.

LECTURE IX— ATTENTION

"Their attention must be gained, or nothing can be done with them."

A primary hindrance to the audience's attention is stuffy sanctuaries. Open the windows and let in fresh air! When the deacons refused to do so at his Park Street Chapel, Spurgeon admitted that he broke them apart.

People often need to be taught to pay attention to the preacher, rather than to each other. Spurgeon would do so on occasion.

The most basic rule is, give them something worth having. Organize your sermon in an orderly, logical manner. Speak plainly in phrases that the hearers can comprehend. In general, neither reading nor reciting your sermons is best. Prepare your sermons with both study and prayer.

Once attention had been gained, holding it is important.

- Do not make the introduction too long. ("It is always a pity to build a great porch to a little house.")
- Do not overly repeat yourself.
- Do not preach too long: forty to forty-five minutes should be the limit.

In his lectures, Spurgeon would repeatedly emphasize the need for illustrations. When asked where they could find illustrations, he replied that there were a hundred illustrations in a single candle. When his students doubted him on this, he took up the challenge and the result was a book, *Sermons in Candles*.

- Be interested yourself. If you are not convinced of the importance of your messages, how can you expect your people to be so?
- Illustrate!
- Pause periodically. ("Speech is silver, but silence is golden when hearers are inattentive.")

Be yourself clothed with the Spirit of God. Do all that you can in preparation, but nothing can take the place of supernatural unction. When God speaks through His servant, people cannot help but listen.

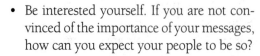

COMMENTARY

For two thousand years, preaching has played a central role in Christianity. Jesus "came preaching" to the multitude; the Apostle "went forth and preached everywhere."

"Ten minutes are too short and forty minutes are too long."—John R. Stott

"Sermonettes are preached by preacherettes and produce Christianettes." —Vance Havner

"If we pastors are going to spend our lives telling the old, old story, maybe we ought to develop our wit as storytellers." —Calvin Miller

The twentieth century has seen the degeneration of preaching and of preachers for several reasons. John Stott in his book, *Between Two Worlds*, suggests three reasons: (1) an anti-authority spirit; (2) the effects of television—physical laziness, intellectual gullibility, and psychological confusion, to name a few; and (3) doubts about the message. These have worked together to produce dumb preachers and deaf congregations.

Yet, preaching remains central to the worship of the church and the evangelization of the lost. Religious television has seen the expansion of preaching, not its demise. Today's megachurches are built around dynamic preachers.

Nevertheless, things have changed. Forty-minute sermons are relatively rare. Television has reduced the attention span of most to twenty to thirty minutes.

A visual generation has arisen that wants to see as well as hear. Points are often made through the help of video clips or dramatic sketches. Providing the congregation with an outline of the sermon often is good, if only to assure them there is a logical sequence and that there is an eventual end to it all.

"Churches are not to be held together except by an instructive ministry; a mere filling-up of time with oratory will not suffice. Everywhere men ask to be fed, really fed."—Charles Haddon Spurgeon

LECTURE X— THE FACULTY OF IMPROMPTU SPEECH

Spurgeon recommended that no man attempt preaching in this style as a general rule.

The Holy Spirit will never do for us what we can do for ourselves. If we can study and do not, we have no right to expect God to make up for our laziness.

"I would have all lazy students drummed out of college; all lazy ministers drummed out of the Assembly." —Alexander Whyte

Write your sermons out, but do not read them from the pulpit or memorize them and recite the words by heart.

The nature of the pastorate is such that the pastor will often be called upon to speak without proper preparation. It is critical, then, that the pastor be well read, a student. A fresh and fertile mind also is invaluable.

Be careful to select a topic with which you are familiar. Spurgeon developed the art of extemporaneous speaking by leading his Monday evening prayer meeting without specific preparation. He said, "Good impromptu speech is just the utterance of a practiced thinker—a man of information, meditating on his legs, and allowing his thoughts to march through his mouth into the open air."

Cultivate a childlike reliance upon the assistance of the Holy Spirit. When emergencies require extemporaneous speaking, rest assured God will aid.

Above all, beware of letting your tongue outrun your brain.

COMMENTARY

The demands of the ministry require that the preacher always be prepared to speak. Even extemporaneous words must arise out of a prepared heart and mind. With that in mind, Martyn Lloyd-Jones in *Preaching and Preachers* contends that the preacher must always be preparing. In that sense, he never has a holiday, is never free from his work. Sermons not only rise from the text, but also are filtered through the thought and personality of the preacher and that process must never be allowed to go stale or stagnate.

LECTURE XI—
THE MINISTER'S FAINTING FITS

"Fits of depression come over most of us."

Mentioning only Luther as an example, Spurgeon goes on to list reasons why pastors are prone to fits of melancholy and depression.

- Pastors are men. Sorrow and affliction are integral parts of the human condition, and pastors are not immune. The experience of trials enable pastors to empathize with the people of their congregation.

- Most of us are afflicted with some physical malady, which contributes to our depression. Others are emotionally prone to melancholy. Often this is not a detriment to one's ministry, but a help. At times, pain can produce genius. Jeremiah was as much a prophet as Isaiah.

- The nature of the ministry makes a pastor particularly vulnerable to depression. To plead for souls and see them reject the truth, to bear the burdens of the entire congregation, to see believers fall into sin—these are concerns which can drive the strongest to depression and despair.

- The position of pastor is conducive to loneliness. There are burdens which a pastor cannot share with others but must bear alone.

- A sedentary lifestyle also can lead to melancholy. While artisans give careful attention to the tools of their trade, those who earn their livelihood by mental activity neglect their bodies, continuing to study in stuffy

One of the secrets of Alexander the Great's military genius was the Macedonian Phalanx. The primary precept was, "Never go into battle without the man beside you."

rooms with little or no exercise. A walk in the woods, a day at the beach would do much to lift and renew the mind.

Spurgeon then addresses the seasons when pastors are most prone to depression.

"Whirled from off our feet by a revival, carried aloft by popularity, exalted by success in soul-winning, we should be as the chaff which the wind driveth away, were it not that the gracious discipline of mercy breaks the ship of our vain glory with a strong eastwind, and casts us shipwrecked, naked and forlorn, upon the Rock of Ages."

- It is at the hour of great success. As long as we labor in the struggle, God's grace sustains us. But once victory is achieved, the natural letdown results in melancholy. Witness Elijah after the victory on Mt. Carmel, contemplating suicide under the juniper tree; Jacob, walking with a limp after wrestling all night; Paul, after being caught up in the third heaven, left with a thorn in the flesh. God balances our victories with periods of melancholy so we will constantly depend on His grace.

- Depression occurs before any great undertaking. Confronted with great obstacles, our hearts often fail within us. Soon after coming to London, Spurgeon filled with a sense of his own unfitness, dreaded the work, and floundered in fearfulness.

- Depression happens during a long, unbroken stretch of labor. It is easy for the minister to refuse the rest which God intended for all. Sundays surely are not restful for pastors.

After his initial breakdown in 1856 from the Surrey Music Hall tragedy, Spurgeon regularly spent four to six weeks a year in Mestone in the south of France to escape the chill and damp of England as well as the pressures of ministry.

- Depression results when one has been cruelly disappointed or hurt. Who has not been betrayed by someone he thought to be a friend? Who has not been disappointed by the moral or spiritual failure of those he thought were sound in their faith?

- Depression comes when troubles multiply. Accumulated problems can wear down even the most determined constitution.

- Some depression comes without a known cause and when least expected. To those who need a cause for every effect, this form of melancholy is particularly disturbing, but nonetheless real.

Do not be overly dismayed when fainting fits strike. They are part of the ordinary ministerial experience.

COMMENTARY

This chapter is undoubtedly the most practical, instructive, and unique of Spurgeon's lectures. Few preachers ever acknowledge depression, much less admit to suffering from it themselves. Spurgeon's transparency and candidness are refreshing.

At the end of the twentieth century, the pastoral ministry has become a minefield of ministerial burnout. One denomination alone estimated that six thousand pastors a year either quit or are fired. One poll indicated that seventy percent of pastors have a lower self-image now than when they began their ministry.

Spurgeon identified the problem and its cause a century before the evangelical world woke up to the situation.

Regarding sedentary lifestyles, it is now known that the brain only comprises two percent of the body's weight but uses forty percent of its oxygen. The primary means of replenishing that oxygen supply is through aerobic exercise. For one whose profession requires much thinking, to remain in a stuffy office without regular exercise is the same as a carpenter or mechanic refusing to sharpen or clean his tools. One of the dangers of ministry is the tendency for our souls to write checks that our bodies cannot cash.

Isolation from others is one of the constant factors in ministerial burnout according to Archibald Hart of Fuller Seminary. According to Hart, the *"Four A's of Burnout"* are: (1) Arrogance—"I don't need accountability"; (2) Addiction—compulsive workaholism; (3) Aloneness—cut off from others; and (4) Adultery—as an artificial substitute for intimacy and satisfaction. Feed these character flaws with the stress of ministry, and burnout (or breakdown) is virtually inevitable.

To summarize Spurgeon: To avoid total burnout, recognize your humanity and expect periods of depression; take good care of your health, and exercise; seek out friends with whom you can confide; and be aware of the various times when melancholy is more prone to occur.

Concerning the loneliness of the pastorate, one poll found that seventy percent of pastors do not have a close friend.

LECTURE XII—THE MINISTER'S ORDINARY CONVERSATION

"We must have humanity along with our divinity if we would win the masses."

By "conversation" Spurgeon meant the entirety of one's manner of living. The issue is how the pastor should conduct himself when he is out of the pulpit.

"There is such a thing as trying to be too much a minister, and becoming too little a man."

- Avoid being ministerially pretentious, stuffy, or stilted.
- Still, a minister can never forget, wherever he might be, that he is still a minister. In a

sense, he is never off duty. Certainly, one must never engage in activities that would bring disrepute to the ministry.

- Be sociable, not a recluse, mingling freely with the people one ministers to and among whom the minister is counted. One of the best signs of a man's character is whether or not children are drawn to him. They are excellent judges of humankind.

- The minister must be cheerful. A general, happy spirit is far more alluring to the lost and saved alike than a melancholy disposition.

- Take care not to dominate all the conversation. Take care to listen to others. Hero worship must never be encouraged. The higher the pedestal one allows his congregation to place him upon, the greater the eventual fall will be. Share in the general conversation and do your best to steer it to profitable purpose.

- Do not frequent parlors, parties, or entertainment merely to gain the favor of influential people. Neglecting the study to attend the parlor is criminal. If you would reach the gentlemanly classes, be a gentleman without pandering to them. In a word: be proper.

- When controversy arises, be gentle in your disposition. Try to avoid debating with people. If you cannot win people by sound argument, do so by an agreeable demeanor.

- When the opportunity arises, speak boldly for one's principles. Take every opportunity to speak out for the Truth. Do not sacrifice your testimony for the sake of amiability.

"An individual who has no geniality about him had better be an undertaker, and bury the dead, for he will never succeed in influencing the living. . . . A man must have a great heart if he would have a great congregation."

COMMENTARY

The pastor's conduct outside the pulpit will arise from his character. The success Spurgeon enjoyed came not only from his earnestness, but also from his genuineness. He disdained to pretend to be anything he was not.

Spurgeon was sociable and congenial. He loved to laugh and make others laugh. He refused to put on airs. A story goes that Dwight L. Moody, the famous American evangelist who came to London to conduct a crusade, wanted to meet Spurgeon face-to-face. Moody went to Spurgeon's home in Norwood and knocked on the door. To his shock, Spurgeon answered the knock with a cigar in his hand—a vice he greatly enjoyed and received much comfort from when the pain of his gout became unbearable.

Moody stammered, "How can a man of God like you have something as vile as that?" as he pointed to the cigar.

William Gladstone (1809–98). Liberal Prime Minister, 1868–74, 1880–85, 1886, and 1892–94, who brought many reforms to Middle-Class England. Benjamin Disraeli (1804–81). Conservative Prime Minister, 1868 and 1874–80, who saved the Conservative Party by wedding it to the interests of the working class.

Spurgeon replied by pointing to Moody's more than ample belly and asked, "And how can a man of God like you possess something as sinful as that?"

William Gladstone and Benjamin Disraeli were the two great rival Prime Ministers of the Victorian Era. A story told about them illustrates the importance of listening. Of Gladstone, it was said if you spent an evening with him, you would leave with the impression that Gladstone was the greatest person alive. However, if you spent an evening with Disraeli, you would leave with the impression that *you* were the greatest person alive.

We should keep in mind that Spurgeon's description of the attitudes and activities of the minister in his casual times is a description of his own style and character. A person might ask whether God cannot use all kinds of people in the service of His kingdom? Does being naturally shy or melancholy disqualify a person from the ministry? Was not Jeremiah both of these, yet greatly used of God? Could not the same be said about Moses? Amos?

LECTURE XIII—TO WORKERS WITH SLENDER APPARATUS

"A good library should be looked upon as an indispensable part of church furniture."

(In this lecture title Spurgeon referred to those ministers with few books and no means to purchase more.)

Spurgeon called upon the deacons of the church whose business it is to "serve tables," to see that the minister's study table is as well stocked as the Communion table and the table of the poor. If the congregation wants better sermons, let them provide better books to their pastors.

- If one cannot spend much, let him spend well. Buy only the best books.
- Master those books which you do have. Re-read them and take notes. "Much not many."
- Borrow good books from friends. Be sure to return all borrowed books.
- Be a master of one book you can never do without—the Bible.

- Make up for a lack of books by spending much time in thought. Thinking is better than possessing many books. Thought is the backbone of study.
- Learn much by merely being observant, especially of nature.
- Study yourself. The most difficult book you will ever read is your own heart.
- Study other people. Become an expert in human nature.
- Learn from older, experienced believers.
- Learn much from inquiring souls.
- Learn much from people as they lie dying. This ultimate moment of truth can be most instructive.

COMMENTARY

Spurgeon was a voracious reader whose personal library held more than twenty-five thousand volumes. He did not take this invaluable resource for granted. Having come from lower-middle-class roots, he knew well the financial difficulties of county preachers. That understanding is the reason for this chapter.

Paper was once taxed in England. Gladstone called it a "tax on knowledge," and managed to get it removed in 1861. With the repeal of this tax, which had made books and newspapers too expensive for many, affordable literature was more available to the masses.

To see that the right kind of literature reached the people, Spurgeon formed the Colportage Society in 1866. Sparsely paid men would wander through the slums offering religious literature at reduced prices. Spurgeon's homebound wife, Susannah, took it upon herself to administer this ministry. By 1890, ninety-five workers sold over 340,000 books and 395,000 periodicals, mostly to the poorest of people.

If the writer of Proverbs felt compelled to urge all believers never to stop growing in wisdom and knowledge, how much more crucial it is for those who would teach and preach to others!

LECTURE XIV—THE HOLY SPIRIT IN CONNECTION WITH OUR MINISTRY

- - - - -

"We ought to be driven forth with abhorrence from the society of honest men for daring to speak in the name of the Lord if the Spirit of God rests upon us."

The presence and anointing of the Holy Spirit upon one's ministry may appear to be a theological issue, but to Spurgeon it was eminently practical. After disassociating himself from those who claimed to be inspired by the Holy Spirit in their "utterances" (nineteenth-century charismatics), Spurgeon listed eight ways the minister might look for assistance of the Holy Spirit.

- The Holy Spirit is the Spirit of knowledge and the source of truth.
- The Holy Spirit is the Spirit of wisdom and guides us in the proper use of the knowledge we have. The Holy Spirit not only guides us into truth, but also guides us into a proper balance of truth, teaching the whole counsel of God. Wisdom is also needed for the manner in which we present truth to different people.
- The Holy Spirit gives freedom of utterance while preaching. We need the Holy Spirit to keep us from saying what we

"Faithfulness requires us to give them a four-squared gospel, from which nothing is exaggerated and for this much wisdom is requisite."

ought not as well as to empower us to say what we should.

- The Holy Spirit is the source of anointing. As we pray in the Spirit, He breaks our own hearts with the truth of the message and causes us to empathize with the congregation.

- The Holy Spirit brings about the desired change in people's hearts. Our constant desire is to change people's hearts; but only the Spirit can do that.

- The Holy Spirit honors our prayers. Much prayer must accompany earnest preaching.

- As the Spirit of Holiness, He enables us to practice out of the pulpit what we preach in it.

- As the Spirit of Discernment, He gives us a pastoral heart of compassion for our people and discernment how best to minister to their various needs.

"Some of us could honestly say that we are seldom a quarter of an hour without speaking to God."

Spurgeon concluded the lecture by explaining how we can hinder the Holy Spirit in our life and ministry.

- The Holy Spirit is hindered in our lives by a lack of sensitiveness that refuses to respond to His leading.

- A dishonest preacher who doubts the doctrine he declares will never be anointed.

- Pride is always a hindrance to the grace and anointing of the Spirit.

- Laziness will vex the Holy Spirit.

- Neglect of private prayer will ensure the diminishing of the Spirit's power.

 COMMENTARY

Spurgeon was only one voice among many notable preachers in Victorian England. If you were to ask him what made him stand out among the others, surely his own explanation would begin with the presence and power of the Holy Spirit upon his life and ministry. When speaking about the unction of the Spirit, one pastor explained. "I may not know for certain what it is, but I know for sure when someone does not have it."

Spurgeon spoke of the necessity of the Spirit's aid in leading and guiding a congregation. He expressed his disapproval of the dictatorial pastor whose people cower before him in passive submission and who would insist, "I am the most important person in the church."

Yet the evidence is plentiful that Spurgeon ran his Metropolitan Tabernacle with a stern, autocratic hand. When he proposed to the New Park Street Church that they build, he did so by laying down the gauntlet: "Build or I resign; either erect the tabernacle or I become an evangelist." He told the church building committee at their first meeting, "I understand some of you are doubtful, if so, go through that door and stay there." Twelve left. When he asked, "Any more?" Three more left!

He once said, "Lead me not into temptation means to me, bring me not into a committee."

If he found a member of the congregation who differed from the church's basic doctrine or policy, he would simply insist that person leave. For all practical purposes, his word was final.

"I am the captain of this vessel. If there should be a Jonah in the ship, I shall in as efficient a spirit as possible pitch him out."

"It is desirable that the Lord's ministers should be the picked-over men of the church, yes, of the entire universe . . . Therefore, I give you the motto, 'Go forward'."

The shield of Spurgeon's College shows a hand firmly gripping the cross with the phrase: "Et Teneo Et Tenor"—"I hold and am held."

Go forward in mental and educational attainment. As the general population becomes increasingly educated, lack of learning will increasingly hinder the pastor's effectiveness. Be specifically well grounded in the Scriptures and in theology. Continue to develop in all spheres of knowledge. First, acquire knowledge. Then, learn to discriminate the truth from error. Finally, retain and hold firmly to what you have learned.

Go forward in oratorical skills. Anyone who thinks he need not improve his preaching ought to quit altogether. Be clear; obscurity is no indication of depth. Be cogent; decibels are no substitute for content. Be persuasive; learn the art of pleading with man which only comes after much time with the Lord.

Strive to go forward in moral character. All the mental and oratorical abilities will not make up for a flawed character. Self-control of our passions is critical. Pride and self-centeredness will forfeit God's blessing. Learn to control both a fiery temper and a tendency to jest about everything. Cultivate integrity, courage, and zeal.

"Know where Adam left you; know where the Spirit of God has placed you. Do not know either of these exclusively as to forget the other."

Above all, we must grow in spirituality. We must maintain balance between two tendencies: first, those who know the deep depravity of their heart, and second, those who realize the glory of their acceptance in Christ. Beyond all else, know Jesus.

Go forward in actual work. All the knowledge in the world is useless if it does not result in practical labors.

Go forward and consider laboring where no one else has gone. Everyone called into the ministry should consider the call of missions and only remain at home if there are sound reasons for doing so.

 COMMENTARY

The nineteenth century was known as "The Age of Progress." It was the by-word and predominant theme of the times. The Industrial Revolution was bringing the fruits of civilization to the masses. Education reform was bringing knowledge to increasing numbers.

In church history, Kenneth Scott Latourette calls the 19th century "The great Century (of) Unprecedented Expansion," as Christian missions took the gospel to the regions beyond.

Much of Spurgeon's genius was his refusal to relax and rest upon his laurels. His inquisitive mind never stopped acquiring knowledge. His spirit was continually open to new endeavors that could touch the lives of people. Little wonder he should encourage his students to press on in every avenue of ministry—sage advice from one who practiced what he preached.

One reason for Spurgeon's effectiveness was his ability to achieve balance. Two examples are in this chapter. First, in the practical realm is the need for balance between levity on one hand

and heaviness of spirit on the other. Spurgeon was well known both for his humor and for his earnestness. The key is to find the right balance.

The second example is in the theological realm. On one hand were the strict Calvinists from whom Spurgeon arose. They emphasized the depravity and loathsomeness of human nature, and they tended toward strict legalism. On the other hand were those who emphasized the completed work of the Spirit, but tended to talk as if they had ceased to sin. Spurgeon reflected the need for balance when he said, "Do not be too afraid of being too full of the Holy Spirit, but never forget the limitation of human nature in this life." Learn all you can from both schools, but maintain balance.

LECTURE XVI—THE NEED OF DECISION FOR THE TRUTH

"Don't go about the world with your fists doubled up for fighting, carrying a theological revolver in the leg of your trousers. There is no sense in being a sort of doctrinal game-cock, to be carried about to show your spirit, or a terrier of orthodoxy, ready to tackle heterodox rats by the score."

"Some things are true and some are false:—I regard that as an axiom."

Though relativism was increasingly popular, we have a fixed faith to preach with a definite message from God.

Of what truths ought we to be absolutely certain?

- God is. He is the Creator and Sustainer of the universe.
- God's Word, the Bible, is inspired by God and, therefore infallible.
- The Trinity—Father, Son, and Holy Spirit who are distinct persons, yet one God.

- Salvation was achieved by the substitutionary atonement of Christ.
- The Holy Spirit is active in regeneration and empowering believers.
- Salvation requires new birth.
- Sin results in eternal separation from God.
- Salvation is all of grace.
- Justification is by faith alone.

How are we to hold to these infallible truths?

- Do not go looking for a theological fight.
- Let your tone and manners be of utter sincerity and earnestness.
- Let your actions back up your convictions.

Why should we be certain of these truths at this time? Because doubts abound at this time, the progress that dominates popular thinking has brought a loosening from the moorings of faith. The age is very impressionable; therefore, let men of decision do the impressing. The Oxford movement has captured the mind of many, if only because of their sincerity.

Spurgeon said, "How strange it would be to hear a man say, 'I am a servant of the Most High God, and I will go wherever I can get the most salary!'"

The Seminary Axiom: "God is everywhere. Go where the money is."

$\aleph$ COMMENTARY

While Spurgeon's era saw the growth and expansion of the kingdom of God both in England and around the world, he rightly observed that the axe had been laid to the root of Christianity by the spread of theological liberalism.

In theology, this led to the undermining of biblical authority as miracles were categorically denied and foundational doctrines were cast aside. In 1835, David Strauss (1808–1874) shocked the world with his book, *The Life of Jesus*, in which he "demythologized" the Gospels and left only a human shell. Although Strauss was

Strauss boasted, "From this time forward no one will be able to view the life of Christ as anything but a fable." Today, only one out of ten thousand can tell you who David Strauss is, but untold millions know Jesus Christ personally. Strauss' bones are buried under—of all things—a cross!

fired from his position as professor of theology at Tübingen, his heresy gained a wide following.

Spurgeon eventually was led into what has been dubbed the "Downgrade Controversy." First, he publicly objected to the spread of liberalism in his own Baptist Union. Then, he later withdrew from the Union when they refused to deal with the issues. The personal attacks and anguish of soul the controversy caused may have hastened Spurgeon's death. His deep concern that theological erosion would eventually bring about the decline of the church has, unfortunately, proven true in twentieth–century Britain and elsewhere. While this has been a trend in Britain, Western Europe, and North America, there are hopeful countertrends here and there.

"It's quite certain, dear friends, that now or never we must be decided, because the age is manifestly drifting."

LECTURE XVII— OPEN-AIR PREACHING— A SKETCH OF ITS HISTORY

"Not only must something be done to evangelize the millions, but everything must be done, and perhaps amid variety of effort the best thing would be discovered."

Open-air preaching is as old as preaching itself. Perhaps Enoch, the seventh from Adam, preached from a hillside; Noah warned his neighbors in his shipyard; Moses and Joshua preached beneath the open sky; Samuel in the field; Elijah on Mt. Carmel; Jonah in the streets of Ninevah – all were open-air preachers. In the New Testament, John the Baptist preached repentance from the riverbank. Our Lord taught on the mountain and on the plain; and the Apostles spread the news not only in the synagogues, but also in the streets.

In the Middle Ages, the best preachers were the itinerant friars.

When the Reformation began, Wycliffe and Huss were driven from the churches into the open air. Many "gospel oaks" marked the place where banished preachers proclaimed the good news, as the truth was made known to the common people.

During the time of the Puritans, those who had been banished from preaching in the churches took the message out of doors. Gravel pits, woods, and hillside—wherever these persecuted preachers could gather a crowd, they preached.

When George Whitefield was banished from the Church of England in the eighteenth century, he took to the fields. His friend, John Wesley, preached from his father's gravestone for three days to throngs after he was banished from his father's pulpit. For most of the eighteenth century, open-air preachers braved mobs, wild bulls, stonings, and death threats to preach the gospel to those who would not or could not come to church.

Historians agree that the influences of the gospel brought to bear upon the working classes by Whitefield and Wesley helped Britain avert a bloody revolution like the one that tore France apart.

In America, camp meetings of the Second Awakening became a common occurrence. People would spend weeks in the wilderness listening to impassioned preaching from dawn until dusk, and long into the night.

SN COMMENTARY

In 1921, barely two months after becoming the first commercial radio station, KDKA invited the prestigious Calvary Episcopal Church of Pittsburgh, Pennsylvania, to broadcast their services. The pastor refused, claiming, "The airwaves are the devil's territory." Fortunately, the youth pastor saw the possibilities and preached over the radio. Only after it became popular did the pastor take over the program.

One might well wonder what the practical purpose of this historical discourse is. Perhaps Spurgeon's main point is that the gospel must be taken to the masses by whatever means possible. His own preaching career demonstrated this conviction. When New Park Street Church proved incapable of holding the crowds he attracted, Spurgeon rented Exeter Hall where various Christian societies held their annual meetings. As they waited for the Metropolitan Tabernacle to be completed, he spoke in the Surrey Music Hall, which seated twelve thousand. Those who thought he was profaning the gospel by preaching in a place of entertainment criticized him severely. Spurgeon did not care.

The twentieth century has followed in the footsteps of those who spoke in the open-air forum to reach the people. Billy Sunday preached in makeshift tents with sawdust aisles. Billy Graham has preached in the largest athletic stadiums in the world and to over one million at an airport in South Korea. Although we have not all been as ready to use it as we might, the development of technology has aided the spread of the gospel in our century.

Not only radio, but also Christian television now reaches untold millions. Internet web sites are being used to advertise church ministries, and religious "chat rooms" where the gospel is presented and defended, have become the Mars Hill of our age.

" 'If by any means I may save some' must be our motto."

Who will enable us to win theses slums and dens for Jesus? . . . I am persuaded that the more of open-air preaching there is in London, the better."

A person need not defend open-air preaching against those who insist the only proper place for preaching is in hallowed sanctuaries. The only limitation is inclement weather.

"Tents are bad—utterly bad . . . Under canvas the voice is deadened and the labor of speaking greatly increased." The development of amplification has changed that and made tent revivals highly successful.

- The primary benefit of open-air preaching is the ability to reach those who wouldn't darken the door of the church. Take the message to the people! Some are too poorly dressed and groomed to go to church, while others still have misconceptions and misgivings about attending a church service.

- A secondary benefit of open-air preaching is the excitement its novelty engenders among regular churchgoers.

- Choose the spot carefully. A field right next to the chapel is best. One can easily move inside. Spurgeon's favorite open-air setting was a hillside that formed a natural amphitheater. Avoid swampy ground. Preaching into the wind makes it impossible to be heard.

Whitefield supposedly could be heard a mile away. Few people are aware that he would often rupture blood vessels in his throat while preaching.

- The style of preaching in open-air must differ from normal preaching. Avoid verbosity. Use many illustrations with short, simple sentences. Be ready for hecklers.

- Be natural and avoid pretense. Speak to be heard but do not bawl. One would do well to take friends with him to aid and protect.

$\mathbb{S_N}$ COMMENTARY

If illustrations, stories, and direct speech were needed for the streets of London in the nineteenth century, they are essential for the average pulpit in the twentieth.

Ours is a visual, interactive generation. From the grasslands of African mission endeavors to the average congregation in the Bible Belt, people learn by hearing stories of the truth.

Beyond that, people now want to see the truth in action. Drama teams and video clips are used increasingly to get the message across because the more of the five senses one can engage, the more impact the message has. Perhaps our Lord had this in mind when He established the Lord's Supper to commemorate the central truth of Calvary. We hear it, see it, touch it, smell it and taste it.

Spurgeon was an innovator, willing to do whatever it took—short of tampering with the truth—to reach people for Christ. His own Metropolitan Tabernacle sat nearly five thousand and overflow crowds packed it several times a week.

LECTURE XIX— POSTURE, ACTION, GESTURE, ETC. (#1)

"The sermon itself is the main thing . . . (However), little oddities and absurdities of mode and gestures which wise men would endeavor not to notice are not overlooked by the general public. . ."

It is not so much developing the right actions, as it is getting rid of those that distract from the message. Better to stand stock still as a statue, like Ulysses of old, than to gesture awkwardly.

Sometimes awkwardness comes naturally. A person raised behind a mule, walking in a plow furrow, will have to train hard to learn to walk without a telltale gait.

Awkward gestures often arise from nervousness or a lack of confidence. These, however, can be overcome with practice.

Victorian pulpits contribute to sermonic awkwardness, hemming the speaker in, constricting his freedom and hiding all but his head and shoulders. These pulpits are little more than coffins set on end.

Many are made awkward because of fear. Practice and becoming familiar with your congregation are great remedies for this cause of awkwardness.

Some oddities occur while searching for the next word.

Bad habits become nearly impossible to break. One speaker would wind and unwind a thread

"Let a man get on fire for God, and people will come to watch him burn."
John Wesley

"Stand upright, get a firm position, and then speak like a man."

while he spoke. Another would tug on a button or twiddle his fingers.

Posture should be natural, but not coarse. Avoid bending, slouching, lolling, or sprawling.

The general rule about action is that it should be natural and never excessive. Of all Europeans, Englishmen are the least demonstrative in their speech. It is best when actions are scarcely noticeable at all.

However, action should be expressive and appropriate. Gestures should correspond to the speaker's thoughts—unlike the ancient Greek orator who exclaimed, "O Heaven!" while pointing to the earth. In the same fashion, a preacher quoted, "Come unto me," with fists clinched in a pugnacious stance! Look upon your people as you preach to them.

 COMMENTARY

At least one poll has found that the number one fear of modern adults is that of having to stand before people and speak. The awkward movements and gestures of many public speakers seem to underscore this truth. The place and nature of the pulpit in Christian history is an apt description of the style of preaching that has developed through the centuries. There was little use of a pulpit in the earliest times—from the mountainside in Galilee where our Lord explained the nature of the kingdom, to Mars Hill in Athens where Paul reasoned with the philosophers.

The pulpit was nearly banished in the Middle Ages, when the mass became the focal point of worship. During Reformation times, the pulpit reappeared, but off to the side, usually high above the people. In the last quarter of the twentieth century, pulpits have shrunk to little more than lecterns upon which to place notes. Some are even transparent plastic to reduce the separation between the preacher and his congregation altogether. Increasingly, pulpits are removed altogether as pastors speak without notes, pacing not just across the platform, but even among the people. The practice seems to have come full circle.

LECTURE XX— POSTURE, ACTION, GESTURE, ETC. (#2)

". . . we have said that gesture should not be excessive, and secondly that it should be appropriate: now comes the third canon, action should not be grotesque."*

Spurgeon gave the following examples of "grotesque action:"

- Those who are stiff. These are the ones whose joints appear rigid and frozen for whatever reason.
- Those who are regular and mechanical. These are the ones whose movements are prescribed like those of a machine. First one hand chops the air, then the other, whether called for or not. It is time for another gesture. First, turn to the left for thirty seconds; then to the right. Others pound the pulpit with fierce regularity, if not with any reason or sense.

- Those who are the laborious. These are the ones who mount the pulpit determined to have it out with the devil or the unfortunate congregation—physically as well as verbally—believing frenzy to be an apt substitution for logic and unction.

- Those who are self–impressed. Almost the opposite of the laborious, there are those self–styled golden throats who utter a few common platitudes. Then, with the air of one who has out–preached Chrysostom, they pause for the audience to express their delirious approval. While nothing profound has been said, only the speaker is unaware of the fact.

- Those who are the martial. These are the ones whose every sermon involves fighting the good fight. Their attitude is argumentative; their actions are hostile.

- Those who are ill–timed. These are the ones whose gestures do not accompany the words. It is as though they speak the thought, then remember a gesture was needed, then provide it, and then go on incongruously.

- Those whose gestures are simply ugly. Examples are grasping the rail and squatting down; flapping one's coattails; preaching with one's hands in his trousers; grasping one's lapels like a pompous penguin.

- Those who are super-fine. These pay more attention to style and appearance than to preparation or speech. Every hair is in place. They are bejeweled with rings, scented with the latest cologne, and primped and prissy because they are more concerned about how they look than what they say.

"Manliness must never sacrifice to elegance. Our working classes will never be brought even to consider the truth of Christianity by teachers who are starched and fine."

The final rule regarding action in the pulpit is to be natural. Far better ragged dress and ragged speech with artless gestures that are genuine and earnest, than practiced but phony stage-playing in the pulpit. Spurgeon's main concern is to remove gestures and actions that would detract from the message. After that he insists each person should develop a style that is uniquely his own.

 ## COMMENTARY

We cannot help but wonder how Spurgeon would react to the sight of many modern preachers. Perfectly shorn and elegantly manicured, dressed in the most expensive clothes, these dandies prance and point, posture and primp. Their messages are often "full of sound and fury, signifying nothing," while they periodically pause and beg for responses from their dutiful listeners ("Hello?" or "Help me, somebody!" or "Can I get a witness?").

Thankfully, not all are so graceless and inappropriate. But, what is surely most needed is unction which begins in the prayer closet, proceeds to the study, and bears final fruit in the pulpit.

LECTURE XXI—EARNESTNESS, ITS MARRIAGE AND MAINTENANCE

"If I were asked – 'What in a Christian minister is the most essential quality for securing success?' . . . I should reply, 'earnestness'."

In soul-winning the man who is consumed with passionate zeal will succeed far beyond what his personal skill and training can explain.

- Earnestness is needed first of all in the preparation of sermons. "The pulpit is the Thermopylae of Christendom: there the fight will be won or lost." Visitation may wax and wane, counseling skills may or may not be present, organizational abilities may be lacking, but all is forgiven if there is power in the pulpit. People must be fed.

- Earnestness is needed while actually in the pulpit. If we are not excited about the truth we convey, how will the people be?

- Earnestness in the pulpit must be genuine. It must never be mimicked. It must arise from a sincere heart that is broken over the lostness of men.

Spurgeon listed six ways earnestnestness can be dampened.

- By the daily grind of pastoral ministry. Whether it is the loneliness of a village pastorate or the demands of a busy city parish, one's zeal can flag under the daily stress lengthened out over the years.

Thermopylae is the pass in northern Greece where a handful of Spartans held off the mighty hordes of the Persians in 480 B.C.

- By the neglect of study. If the preacher is not well–fed spiritually, he will have little fire for the battle of ministry.

- By too much study. It is possible to bury the Spirit under ancient languages and historical analysis.

- By too much frivolity.

- By too much contact with cold Christians. These are self–appointed Cold–Water Committees whose only concern about your preaching is how long it lasts. These arrive late, dare you to get their attention, and leave with a critical attitude.

- By neglect of one's physical needs. Eating too much before preaching, sleeplessness, and sickness all will dampen one's earnestness.

Spurgeon then listed five things a pastor can do to maintain earnestness.

- It must be kindled by the love of Christ. If a man does not have it in the first place, he should not enter the ministry.

- It must be fanned by meditation on the damnable fate of the lost and the glorious destination of the saints.

- Feed the flame by intimate fellowship with Christ by meditation and prayer.

- Earnestness may be maintained by new works of ministry and new courses of study.

- Keep close to the people of your congregation. Be familiar with their joys and sorrows. Be aware of the spiritual needs of your community. Be with them at their deathbeds in order to keep eternity's values in view.

The Puritan, Richard Baxter (1615–91) wrote *The Saints' Everlasting Rest* to help him prepare for death during a life-threatening illness at the age of thirty-five. As he began to meditate on the joys of heaven which he soon expected to enter, he wrote down his thoughts. He eventually recovered and published his reflections in book form."
Timothy K. Beougher

COMMENTARY

Most of Spurgeon's biographers agree that his earnestness was the key to his success with people's hearts. Whether or not one agrees with what he said, there is no doubt Spurgeon believed it, and heaven and hell were at stake in one's response to it. Earnestness. When a century earlier a skeptical philosopher was asked why he went to hear George Whitefield, he replied, "While I don't believe what he says, there is no doubt at all that Whitefield believes it." Earnestness. Ben Franklin was not the only one to flock to Whitefield's meeting only to see him cry. Earnestness.

The so-called Baby Busters and the Generation Xers of our time demand genuineness most of all. They are the most abused, neglected, molested and lied-to generation in history and they loathe the slightest scent of phoniness. If they are to be reached, it will not be by profound or slick oratory; it will be by genuine earnestness for their souls.

Spurgeon felt that too much time in the same location can dampen one's spirit. He quotes Wesley who confesses that if he spent more than one year in the same place, both he and his congregation would be asleep.

Yet, it seems to me that short tenures are the bane of modern pastorates. They are indicative of professional clergy who look upon their flock as stepping-stones in their personal careers. How can the pastor even come to know their names, much less their needs, if he only stays a year or two?

While we all long to see results in our ministry, there is no such thing as greener grass. Jeremiah's weeping for Israel did not lessen because they were unresponsive. Earnestness comes from the heart of one who has spent time with God, not one who is enamored by numerical success.

LECTURE XXII— THE BLIND EYE AND THE DEAF EAR

"You cannot stop people's tongues, and therefore the best thing is to stop your own ears and never mind what is spoken."

In this lecture Spurgeon talked about when the blind eye and deaf ear should be applied.

- Be deaf and blind to differences which were in the church when you came. Do not get involved with one clique or party and sacrifice your ministry to the entire congregation.

- Try to remain aloof from the discussion of finances, especially your own salary. Allow those who are skilled in such things to attend to them.

- Distance yourself from persons who carry gossip. Ask them to write down their comments so you do not forget any detail when you go to the person being gossiped about. Beg your wife also to avoid gossips.

- Beware of becoming suspicious of those who offer constructive criticism.

- It is a serious mistake to assume every honest critic is an enemy.

"Those who praise us are probably as much mistaken as those who abuse us . . . Surely we are not popes, and do not wish our hearers to regard us as infallible."

- Be deaf to any knowledge that was not meant for you.

- Have a blind eye and deaf ear. Do not search out or listen for opinions about you. Repress your curiosity.

- When you are lied about, it is best to turn a deaf ear. Responding to lying reports only fans the flame of gossip. The best answer is a blameless life. Only the most public and deplorable lies should be lies addressed.

- It is best to remain blind and deaf to another church's problems. Do not encourage malcontents to share the faults of their pastor or people.

"A great lie, if unnoticed, is like a big fish out of water, it dashes and plunges and beats itself in a short time."

 COMMENTARY

The wisdom of the chapter is profound and timeless. One of the most important pastoral arts is being able to receive praise and criticism. There is a kernel of truth in even your worst enemy's criticism and a morsel of falsehood in your best friend's praise. Learn to distinguish both and avoid the plague of man-pleasing. Another part of wisdom is realizing that no one can ever be as bad—or as good—as your predecessor in the pulpit.

We must beware how different Spurgeon's views on church finances were from the modern model of minister as chief executive officer, sitting in on every meeting and having the final say on every decision. It is also interesting to note that Spurgeon himself was more like the modern model. He personally raised the funds and oversaw the construction of the Metropolitan Tabernacle. Spurgeon's abilities ensured that his family would never go lacking, but how many impoverished preachers have been forced to plead for an adequate salary with those in charge of finances?

LECTURE XXIII—ON CONVERSION AS OUR AIM

"For the most part, the work of preaching is intended to save the hearers."

Spurgeon's success was due, at least in part, to his ability to keep balance in his life and in his ministry. He begins this chapter by asserting the need to both edify the saints and reach the lost—to preach the whole counsel of God as well as primarily evangelistic messages. Spurgeon made eight points from which the heart of the soul-winner emerges.

"We must see souls born unto God. If we do not, our cry should be that of Rachel—'Give me children or I die.'"

1. We must be careful to depend entirely upon the Spirit of God. This dependence should foster more study and more prayer.

2. We should focus more on the following truths that lead to conversion.

- The person and work of Christ, especially the cross

- The sinfulness of sin and the failure of the law

- Human depravity; the certainty of judgment; the soon coming of Christ

- The substitutionary atonement of Christ; justification by faith alone

- Both the love and justice of God

3. We are to present these truths to them understandably, appealing to their intellect; earnestly, pleading to their emotions;

and even threateningly, warning of judgment to come.

4. Don't always save the evangelistic appeal for the last of the sermon when the lost are least likely to hear and respond.

5. Preach believing; expect and prepare for people to respond. Love the lost to Christ.

6. Be available to talk to inquirers often.

7. Enlist the help of the people. Train them to be soul-winners.

8. Call in outside speakers periodically who have a gift for evangelism.

 COMMENTARY

In Spurgeon's nearly forty years in London, well over fourteen thousand people were converted and baptized in his church. Only God knows how many others were converted as he spoke elsewhere or by reading his sermons.

When young William Carey, the father of modern missions, shared his burden for the lost of Asia with his fellow pastors, he was rebuked by a tired, old hyper–Calvinist with the words, "Young man, if God has chosen the multitudes of Asia, they will be saved without our help." Thankfully Carey and Spurgeon—though Calvinists themselves—rejected this fatalistic perversion.

To the extreme Calvinists of his day, Spurgeon was a heretic for pleading with the lost to be converted. The doctrine of total depravity, which Spurgeon also fervently believed, taught that the lost are dead in their sins. Quickening is a work of God alone. To this Spurgeon replied, "If we are only to bid them to do such things as they are capable of doing without the Spirit of God, we are reduced to mere moralists. If it be absurd to bid the dead sinner believe and live, it is especially vain to bid him consider his state and reflect upon his doom."

And, of course, there is the practical answer: "Those who never exhort sinners are seldom winners of souls."

It is also interesting to note, however, that Spurgeon would appeal to the emotions as well as the intellect of the lost, but he refused to manipulate people into responding. While he pleaded with the people to come to Christ, the "altar call" was a development of the next century. Generally, Spurgeon reserved Tuesday night for inquirers to return to the church for personal counseling. If the Spirit of God was generally at work, He would sustain that work even after the lost had gone home.

Lecture XXIV— Illustrations in Preaching

"Reasons are the pillars of the fabric of a sermon; but similitudes (illustrations) are the windows which give the best lights."—Thomas Fuller

In this lecture Spurgeon made eight important points about illustrating the sermon.

- The primary purpose of an illustration is to let in light or to enhance understanding. If possible, there should be at least one good metaphor in the shortest address.

- Illustrations serve to gain and sustain interest.

- Illustrations should not be too numerous. Although illustrations serve as windows of understanding for a sermon, an all-glass house is not practical.

- Illustrations should not be used as an end in themselves, but to cast light on the truth at hand.

"Let us not deny the salt of a parable with the meat of doctrine. . . Even the little children open their eyes and ears, and a smile brightens up their faces as we tell a story."

- Illustrations should arise naturally from the truths they portray. They should be in touch with things familiar to the listeners.
- Illustrations should be simple and brief, not long and elaborate.
- Illustrations should be in good taste, not low or vulgar. Dirty windows bring a reproach.
- Do not mix metaphors.

A temperance speaker once said, "Comrades, let us be up and doing! Let us take our axes on our shoulders, and plough the waste places till the good ship Temperance sails gaily over the land."

 COMMENTARY

Illustration was one of Spurgeon's greatest oratorical gifts. He was one of the all-time masters. I counted the illustrations, similes, metaphors, allusions and quotations Spurgeon used in this chapter alone and the final tally was over ninety in fourteen pages. Nearly every other sentence contains an illuminating picture, analogy, or simile.

Technology can be a tremendous aid for preaching in our age. One drama or brief video can do more to make the point than hours of exhortation. If "a picture is worth a thousand words," would it not make sense to avail ourselves of videos and overheads to illustrate visibly the truths we are trying to explain?

LECTURE XXV—
ANECDOTES FROM
THE PULPIT

. . . . .

"If they sneer at anecdotes, we smile at them and their sneers, and wish them more sense and less starch."

Spurgeon took hard issue with those who said the use of anecdotes and stories in the pulpit was trite and beneath the dignity of proclaiming divine truth. In this chapter, he gives examples of the great preachers from the Reformation to his day who used stories to illustrate truths in their sermons.

First, God Himself, used histories and biographies throughout Scripture to illustrate divine principles. Christ continually used parables to teach. Is the preacher of the gospel above the One about whom the gospel is centered?

He goes on to give anecdotal examples from the sermons of Hugh Latimer, Thomas Watson (among other Puritans), and George Whitefield of the Great Awakening. He concludes with the American evangelist, D. L. Moody, whom he describes as the "one living man, who, above all others, has in two continents stirred the masses of the people"—an interesting and humble evaluation.

The primary thing is to use stories to illustrate the biblical truths you are declaring without letting the stories become the focus. We are preachers of the gospel, not entertainers; and our purpose is their salvation, not their praise.

COMMENTARY

Recent years have seen the re-emphasis in "storying" from the evangelization of primitive tribes to television preaching. While true preaching must always be biblical in its source and content, the delivery of the message is becoming increasingly anecdotal in our generation.

The effects of television alone have demanded that the present–day preacher use word pictures, if not actual pictures on a screen, to capture and hold the attention of modern-day audiences. Some might object to that demand, but as one person has observed, "These may be the best of times or the worst of times, but they are the only times we have."

In his book, *Spirit, Word, and Story*, Calvin Miller notes that right-brain dominant and relational people need stories they can relate to. Left-brain dominant and didactic people need precepts to give organization and structure to divine truth. Miller contends that both stories and precepts are needed in our sermons. The primary burden of the preacher is to take other-worldly, spiritual truths and relate them to the practical, unspiritual existence of most people.

Anecdotes help to do this, but the stories must be about ultimate, eternal truths that matter.

Perhaps it would be most instructive to observe the preaching style of our Lord as to how much of His sermons was doctrinal precepts, and how much was illustrative and anecdotal. The most doctrinal book of the New Testament, the book of Romans, is only fifty percent doctrinal and the rest is practical application.

LECTURE XXVI—
THE USES OF ANECDOTES
AND ILLUSTRATIONS

Spurgeon commends the methods of the newly established (1878) Salvation Army under the direction of General William Booth (1829–1912). In his efforts to reach the urban poor, Booth formed brass bands that marched through the ghettos calling the masses to Christ.

"We cannot endure a sleepy audience."

Use anecdotes and illustrations *to attract and secure the attention of the audience.* An anecdote in a sermon is like a picture in a book. Common sense will help the preacher suit his speech to his audience. The less instructed, the more the need for anecdotes and illustrations.

One dull preacher watched as every member of the congregation dozed off to sleep except the town idiot. With a roar the preacher woke and scolded them all: "Everyone of you fell asleep except poor Jock, the idiot." To which Jock cried, "And if I had not been an idiot, I should have been asleep too."

Use anecdotes and illustrations *to make your preaching life-like and vivid.* Avoid anything that appears theatrical or phony. Strive for genuineness and simplicity. Jesus spoke with parables from everyday life in a natural tone and manner. Go to the people; reach them as they are, where they are.

Use anecdotes and illustrations *to explain doctrine or make exhortation clear.* In any set of instructions, the most important and helpful part is the diagram. So, too, illustrations clarify the doctrinal truth.

Many of our people cannot grasp logical arguments, but can easily understand the moral of the story. Children especially are better able to grasp truth in story form than in rational

> "The twelfth (commandment) is, 'Thou shalt pull a long face on Sunday.' I must confess that I would rather hear people laugh than I would see them asleep in the house of God; and I would rather get the truth into them through the medium of ridicule than I would have the truth neglected, or leave the people to perish through lack of reception of the truth."

propositions. Humor is especially helpful in getting a point across.

Use anecdotes and illustrations *to help the audience remember the truth being preached*. The human mind will recall the illustration long after the text and its main point are forgotten. Anecdotes leave a longer lasting impression on the mind.

Use anecdotes and illustrations *to aid in arousing the feelings of the audience*. Beware, however, of repeating illustrations, for each time the emotional effect is less.

Use anecdotes and illustrations *to capture the attention of the careless*. The young and the weary must be reached as well as those who are yearning and interested. Stories capture the attention of the most disinterested listeners.

Spurgeon concluded with a warning to be sure that your sermons are not all frothy illustrations and void of content. A lady was asked after church if she thought the sermon had much spirit in it. "Oh yes!" she replied, "it was all spirit; there was no body to it at all."

 COMMENTARY

Part of Spurgeon's genius lay in his ability to illustrate. In these twenty-two pages he makes seven points and manages to illustrate them with fifty-seven stories—not metaphors or similes, but actual illustrative stories.

Recent findings in the area of education show that different people learn in different ways. Some learn by listening and categorizing truth into logical categories while others process information in pictures and can only learn by use of stories.

Spurgeon observed this fact a century before it became established educational doctrine.

While he advocated the liberal use of anecdotes, Spurgeon seemed to disdain the use of object lessons as being "puerile" or childish. With the advent of television, the late twentieth century has become much more visual in its learning. Today visual aids greatly enhance the spoken word and almost are becoming a necessity. As we enter the twenty-first century, electronics will become the standard in aiding communication.

We might be tempted to criticize Spurgeon's use of anecdotes to arouse the emotions of the audience. Our generation has seen the great harm from emotion-arousing demagogues such as Hitler, Mussolini, Jim Jones, and others. We are a bit frightened at the blatant admission that sermons are partially designed to arouse feeling in the listener. But Spurgeon was never satisfied with a strictly rational message. In order to produce genuine conversion, the listener's heart must be appealed to as well as his mind. The key, of course, is balance.

"He has the whole world to go to as a storehouse of illustration."

Spurgeon begins by disdaining anecdotes that might not be true, especially anecdotes from one's imagination. He then provides a number of sources for illustrative material.

- *Current history.* The daily newspaper is filled with stories that are both current and poignant. The day Spurgeon gave this lecture, he read of a terrible shipwreck caused by the lack of lights—an apt illustration of the destruction of the lost through lack of knowledge of Christ.
- *Local history.* Find out the legends and myths of the people to whom you are preaching.
- *Ancient and modern history.* Spurgeon loved to use lessons that ranged from Greek mythology and the classics to modern history. He assumed that ministers were avid readers of history.
- *Religious history.* This was one of Spurgeon's favorite sources of illustration. He especially loved stories from the Reformation and the Puritan era.
- *Natural history.* People tend to respond to illustrations from the world of nature that can be verified by observation. The same God is the Author of both Scriptures and nature. Try to draw from a variety of sciences and sources. The cat that sits in your lap tonight has soft paws but sharp

claws—much like temptation which seems soft and harmless at first, then wounds and scars in the end.

Spurgeon told about seeing the neighborhood mongrel tearing up his garden. He threw his walking stick at it and shouted at it to stay out. The mangy cur picked up the stick in his mouth, brought it to him, and lay it at his feet with tail wagging in eager expectation of gratitude. This changed Spurgeon's attitude toward the mutt. How illustrative of the way a soft answer turns away wrath!

Regularly teaching children is good because children need illustrations and stories to hold their attention.

- *Literature.* Read books that contain illustrations. Words, themselves, with their roots and definitions shed light.
- *The Scriptures.* Scripture is the best commentary on itself. The Old Testament is rich in types, symbols, and stories written for our nurture and admonition.

While Spurgeon disdained making up anecdotes and stories, he urged his students to collect illustrations. It is an art that develops with use.

"Half the battle lies in making the attempt, in coming to the determined resolution, 'God helping me, I will teach the people by parables, by similes, by illustrations, by anything that will be helpful to them; and I will seek to be a thoroughly interesting preacher of the Word.'"

 COMMENTARY

As Spurgeon himself noted, if it behooved Jesus to use parables, similes, and metaphors, we dare not disdain them as a means of making our message clear. Our century's most respected and effective preacher, Billy Graham, is noted for his constant use of current events to bring the timeless truths of Scriptures into relevant relationship to the lives of his audiences.

One problem facing a communicator today is the general cultural illiteracy of the "New Generation." They have no idea who Ulysses and Agamemnon were. The only Napoleon they have heard of plays running back for the Oakland Raiders. While most have been told a good deal about Martin Luther King, few know anything about the original Martin Luther!

If our generation has become culturally and historically illiterate, how much more have they become biblically ignorant. We cannot simply assume they know who Joseph or the patriarchs or David or Pilate were. This generation thinks the epistles may have been the wives of the apostles! We must choose our illustrations from literature or history carefully or we will have to spend too much time explaining the illustration itself. Even local history has its limits. The average American relocates every three years, hardly settling long enough to learn the history and background.

Everyday life, however, is a gold mine of illustrations. The single most influential common denominator of our culture, for better or worse, is television. The younger members of our congregation are far more familiar with the Simpsons than the Psalms. If you are talking about judges, they will take more notice of Judge Wapner than Deborah or Gideon.

We can wail, moan, and rail against the current; or we can adapt our style and use illustrations from contemporary culture that connect with our audiences. As has been noted before—these may be the best of times; they may be the worst of times; but they are the only times we have. While the truth of God's Word is eternal and unchanging, the way we convey it must be adapted to reach our ever-changing congregations.

Lecture XXVIII—Encyclopedias of Anecdotes and Illustrations

· · · · ·

The apostle Paul was a reader. He instructed Timothy from his Roman prison cell to "bring with thee . . . the books, but especially the parchments" (2 Tim. 4:13). Spurgeon believed these may have contained sources of illustrations, for Paul's writings and sermons were replete with them.

In this chapter Spurgeon listed and evaluated a number of books and encyclopedias of illustrations. Virtually all of them are out of print, archaic, and outdated.

The examples he gave in this chapter are still good illustrative material for our generation. Let me give an example: There are times in every believer's life when through trials and afflictions God seems to withdraw His presence and hide His face. Why? Spencer likens it to a tender-hearted father walking through the city with his little son. The boy, enthralled by the sights, runs ahead and lingers behind and soon becomes more thrilled at the sights than content with the father. So the father hides behind a post or around a corner until the child realizes his aloneness and cries out for his father. The end result is a closer walk and a deeper relationship. Truths like that are timeless.

Spurgeon complained lightly how many of his anecdotes and illustrations showed up in these

Consider his favorite source: *Things New and Old; or A Storehouse of Similes, Sentences, Allegories, Apophthegms, Apologies, Adages, Divine, Moral, Political, etc.; Writings and Sayings of the Learned in All Ages to the Present* by Spencer. (He does not offer his first name.) This 1,112-page tome was first published in 1658, and some of Spurgeon's students complained about the outdated nature of the anecdotes. Spurgeon recognized this, but insisted that, with a little editing and updating, many of the illustrations could still be useful.

Spurgeon complained that one Church of England writer compiled a volume, quoting him often. By the time the second volume came out, however, Spurgeon had been embroiled in the baptismal regeneration controversy in which he publicly took issue with the Anglicans. So, while the author continued to catalog Spurgeon's illustrations, he inserted them without revealing the source! One Anglican plagiarized him shamelessly and merely attributed the source as an "Old Author"!

collections. Bad enough that he received no royalties, but at least credit was generally given. Spurgeon's own *Feathers for Arrows*, *John Ploughman's Talks* and *Sermons in Candles* are still valuable sources of illustrations today.

 COMMENTARY

Truth is timeless; human nature is unchanging. While the technological details of our lives are ever in flux, some principles transcend the generations and many illustrations shed common light across the ages. Many written collections are available today because preachers always need pertinent anecdotes. Professional journals are incomplete without a section of "Illustrations." Scores of sources are available by subscription. The Internet now makes available thousands of illustrations duly categorized and cross-referenced.

Preachers still must read, evaluate, edit and adapt. This calls for a commitment of time and effort, but the dividends are well worth it.

Lecture XXIX—Books of Fables, Emblems, and Parables

". . . the teaching of God Himself was always mainly by parable."

The Old Testament is filled with parabolic symbols of divine truth. All the sacrifices and ceremonies pointed to deeper lessons. The lamb slain, the blood sprinkled, the first-born killed, the scapegoat sent away, the brazen serpent uplifted are all examples of parables, symbols, and types. Many of the prophets were instructed to give object lessons as visible testimonies to God's warning. Jeremiah wore a yoke, observed the potter, buried the girdle. Hosea married a prostitute, then brought his wayward wife back. Jesus Himself spoke to the people in parables, continually. Should His followers hesitate to do likewise?

Spurgeon warned against using myths because they tend to be taken as fact, and many people lose the deeper truth of the tale.

- Allegories make characteristics into persons and should be used sparingly. Spurgeon himself seldom used allegories.
- Fables are obviously false stories of earthly things meant to depict a deeper truth. It is obvious that the cock did not actually speak to the bull, or that the fox did not offer his sage advice. Because of this, Spurgeon warned against overuse of fables. Yet, Luther claimed to value Aesop's fables second only to the Bible as a source of truth and wisdom. Even Spurgeon recommends Aesop.

The remainder of this chapter quotes extensively from various works—most of which are now obscure—to give examples of myths, allegories, and anecdotes that bear spiritual truth.

When our Lord sat down for the last time with His small band of disciples, He recognized that this band of "slow learners" might forget much He had done and said. He urged them never to forget what He was about to do for them on Calvary's cross and its significance. When He told them to "do this in remembrance of me," he gave them bread and wine which they could touch with their hands, smell, see and taste, all the while telling (hearing) the significance of it all. "This is my body . . . blood . . . for you." When Christ wanted the most essential truth to make the greatest impact, He made sure that the people He was speaking to and instructing involved all five senses.

COMMENTARY

Spurgeon's beloved Puritans were masters at allegory and typology and resorted to that style of preaching. Their influence on his preaching was enormous. He, like they, was much more prone to expound on the typological or allegorical truths he found in Scripture, nature, and history. His favorite was John Bunyan's *Pilgrims Progress*, which is one continual allegory. Only the Bible itself was more influential in his writing and preaching.

It seems that Spurgeon would have liked to use object lessons in his preaching, much like the Old Testament prophets did. But the limited idea of what was proper for preachers in his day kept him from doing so.

Recent findings in the science of learning and education show that the more senses we can involve in our teaching/preaching, the greater will be the impact on our congregations. Many today learn by seeing more than hearing. Others learn by doing. The impact of drama and video in churches today are an indication of this reality. In reality, are we not returning to the methods of the Old Testament prophets?

Lecture XXX—The Sciences as Sources of Illustration

"It seems to me that every student for the Christian ministry ought to know at least something of every science."

God has made everything in the world to be our teacher, and our curriculum is incomplete if we do not learn from the world of nature. Spurgeon confined the entire chapter to the science of astronomy and the many wonders and lessons we can learn from it. He believed that astronomy brings us closer to God than any other science. Surely, "the undevout astronomer is mad."

The telescope is to the astronomer what the Scriptures are to the believer. Neither make truth, but reveal it. African natives commented on Dr. David Livingstone's use of a sextant to make his way across uncharted Africa. They said he could bring down the sun and carry it under his arm. In like manner, faith in the gospel has brought down to us the Father, Son, and Holy Spirit to possess for an eternal joy.

Spurgeon said the pre-Copernican worldview that the earth was the center of the universe was like man-centered theological systems. Both are patently erroneous. The essence of the doctrine of grace is that God is the center, the starting point of all truth, the initiator of every good work.

Spurgeon continued by relating various astronomic facts and drawing the spiritual truth each exemplified.

David Livingstone (1813–73) was a Scottish missionary and explorer who opened up the interior of Africa, heretofore known as "the white man's grave." A legendary Victorian hero, he died in Africa and had his heart buried there while his body was later entombed in Westminster Abbey.

"You have discovered the right form of Christian doctrine when you have found the system that has God in the centre, ruling and controlling according to the good pleasure of his will."

THE SUN

The fact that one cannot look directly at the sun without soon going blind illustrates man's need of a mediator, and how necessary it is to see God through the person of Jesus Christ.

Just as plants need the light of the sun to grow healthy and strong, so too we need the light of God's countenance, without which we shrivel and die. Quoting from the hymn writer Isaac Watts:

> "In darkest shades if he appear,
> My dawning is begun;
> He is my soul's sweet morning star,
> And he is my rising sun."

As a magnifying glass can capture the sun's rays and start a flame, even the hardest sinner's heart will melt if our preaching focuses the truth of the gospel on it.

As the sun is never more observed than when it is eclipsed, so God is never more alluring than when He is suspended on the cross in agony and death. Do not fail to speak continually of the awful eclipse of Calvary.

MERCURY

That planet nearest the sun orbits at the fastest rate and receives the fiercest rays. It is the densest of the planets in order to endure the pace. God fits every man for the race He has ordained for him.

VENUS

Venus is known as the morning star and the "star of the evening." Our Lord is also referred to as the "bright and morning star" who is the harbinger of everlasting light.

EARTH

Though it may appear that we are standing still, we actually are orbiting the sun at a rate of sixty-five thousand miles per hour. Likewise, though it may appear that we are making little progress in our spiritual growth, we often are unaware of the growth God is producing.

Spurgeon goes on to comment briefly about the moon and the other planets known to man in his day, drawing spiritual analogies in each case.

 COMMENTARY

Spurgeon's breadth of knowledge is exemplified in this last chapter. He obviously was widely read in the sciences of his day but never attempted to impress his hearers with his own brilliance. Spurgeon's genius was the ability to extract spiritual truth from virtually any piece of information. He saw the hand of God in everything he gazed upon. His familiarity with the spiritual truths of God's word enabled him to see divine revelation in all the facts of nature and history alike.

QUESTIONS FOR DISCUSSION

1. What, in Spurgeon's opinion, constituted a call to ministry? What might disqualify a person?

2. How important was prayer to Spurgeon in regards to the preacher's ministry? Why was it needful? When was it needful? How did private prayer differ from public prayer?

3. One of the significant aspects of Spurgeon's ministry was balance. How did this manifest itself in the following areas:

- Calvinistic doctrine and evangelistic enthusiasm?

- Unwavering commitment to truth and willingness to try new methods?

- Dependence upon God and personal diligence in all things?

- The need for propriety and for genuine authenticity?

4. One of the most significant chapters is "The Minister's Fainting Fits." Why are ministers prone to fits of depression? When are they most prone? What are some of his suggestions for dealing with melancholy?

5. Spurgeon advocated diligent study and practiced it himself. Why is study so important to the ministry? What areas should be the objects of our study? When a person's resources limit him from purchasing books, what should he do?

6. Spurgeon's theology was foundational to his ministry. What were the unalterable, absolute truths that he held? Among these, what were the major themes of his preaching?

7. Spurgeon believed that earnestness was the most essential quality for success in the ministry. How did this characteristic manifest itself in his prayers, his preparation, his preaching, and his personal life? How can a person hinder or help the level of earnestness in his ministry?

8. One of Spurgeon's greatest gifts was the power of illustration. Why did he feel illustrations were so important? Where can a person find illustrations? What are some guidelines in using illustration?

"Compel Them to Come In" (*Luke 14:23*)

Delivered Sunday a.m., December 6, 1858, at Sunny Gardens Music Hall

BACKGROUND INFORMATION

W. Y. Fullerton in his biography of Spurgeon (1920) claims that this particular sermon is the one "to which the greatest testimony has been borne of converting power. . . . It is said that some hundreds joined the church as a result of its influence, and from the ends of the earth scores of others have declared it was their means of salvation."

In London, Spurgeon was riding the crest of popularity—or infamy, depending on one's opinion. New Park Street Church could not hold the throngs who clamored to hear the young preacher. So the Royal Music Hall in Sunny Gardens was rented. It seated eight thousand people and had room for five thousand more to stand. The first service, October 19, 1856, was a tragic fiasco. Twenty-two thousand were present and someone shouted "Fire!" The resulting panic caused seven deaths and many injuries.

Spurgeon was heart-broken by grief and the vilification of the press. But he soon recovered to preach for years in the Music Hall to thousands of Londoners from all walks of life—from politicians to prostitutes, merchants to maids, princes to pickpockets. These were the evangelistic sermons of his ministry and, as a result, thousands were won to the cause of Christ.

Imagine the scene! Thirteen thousand eager, excited people were inside while several

The year was 1858. Revival had broken out the previous year in America and had leaped across the Atlantic. It was a phenomenal season of harvesting of souls.

Notice the Reformed theology that begins with God's holiness and man's sinfulness. Yet Spurgeon keeps things in balance: God's justice is balanced by His mercy. Halfway through the sermon he will take issue with hyper-Calvinists who might criticize him for pleading with the lost, but plead with them he does. At the conclusion, his entreaties ended, he rests the matter in the Master's hands.

Reformed in its theology, the emphasis of Spurgeon's message was christological. Notice the language of Nicea—very God of very God—in Spurgeon's reference to the person and work of Christ.

thousand more waited eagerly on the outside to get in and hear the message.

And what is it? "Compel them to come in!"

The Message
"Compel them to come in."—Luke 14:23

I feel in such a haste to go out and obey this commandment this morning, by compelling those to come in who are now tarrying in the highways and hedges, that I cannot wait for an introduction, but must at once set about my business.

The Audience
Hear then, O ye that are strangers to the truth as it is in Jesus—hear then the message that I have to bring you. Ye have fallen, fallen in your father Adam; ye have fallen also in yourselves, by your daily sin and your constant iniquity; you have provoked the anger of the Most High; and as assuredly as you have sinned, so certainly must God punish you if you persevere in your iniquity, for the Lord is a God of justice, and will by no means spare the guilty. But have you not heard, hath it not long been spoken in your ears, that God, in his infinite mercy, has devised a way whereby, without any infringement upon his honour, he can have mercy upon you, the guilty and the undeserving? To you I speak; and my voice is unto you, O sons of men.

The Savior
Jesus Christ, very God of very God, hath descended from heaven, and was made in the likeness of sinful flesh.

Begotten of the Holy Ghost, he was born of the Virgin Mary; he lived in this world a life of exemplary holiness, and of the deepest suffering, till at last he gave himself up to die for our sins, "the just for the unjust, to bring us to God."

The Call

And now the plan of salvation is simply declared unto you—"Whosoever believeth in the Lord Jesus Christ shall be saved." For you who have violated all the precepts of God, and have disdained his mercy and dared his vengeance, there is yet mercy proclaimed, for "whosoever calleth upon the name of the Lord shall be saved." "For this is a faithful saying and worthy of all acceptation, that Christ Jesus came into the world to save sinners, of whom I am chief;" "whosoever cometh unto him he will in no wise cast out, for he is able also to save unto the uttermost them that come unto God by him, seeing he ever liveth to make intercession for us." Now all that God asks of you—and this he gives you—is that you will simply look at his bleeding, dying son, and trust your souls in the hands of him whose name alone can save from death and hell. Is it not a marvelous thing, that the proclamation of this gospel does not receive the unanimous consent of men? One would think that as soon as ever this was preached, "That whosoever believeth shall have eternal life," every one of you, "casting away every man his sins and his iniquities," would lay hold on Jesus Christ, and look alone to his cross. But alas! such is the desperate evil of our nature, such the pernicious depravity of our character, that this message is despised, the invitation to the gospel feast is rejected, and there are many of you who are this day enemies of God by wicked works, enemies to the God who preaches Christ to you today, enemies to him who sent his Son to give his life a ransom for many. Strange I say it is that it should be so, yet nevertheless it is the fact, and hence the necessity for the command of the text,—"Compel them to come in." Children of God, ye who have

Spurgeon quotes thirty-six Scripture passages in this sermon—all the more remarkable since his preaching was almost completely extemporaneous. Just the roughest outline notes were taken into the pulpit.

"Simply look." Spurgeon was converted when a layman pleaded with him from Isaiah 45:22: "Look unto me and be ye saved."

Someone has recommended preachers to "(1) tell them what you are about to say, (2) say it, and (3) tell them what you have said." Spurgeon explains his primary outline here.

How do poverty and poverty of spirit prepare a person to receive Christ?

believed, I shall have little or nothing to say to you this morning; I am going straight to my business—I am going after those that will not come—those that are in the byways and hedges, and God going with me, it is my duty now to fulfil this command, "Compel them to come in."

Those Called

First, I must *find you out;* secondly, I will go to work to *compel you to come in.* If you read the verses that precede the text, you will find an amplification of this command: "Go out quickly into the streets and lanes of the city, and bring in hither the poor, the maimed, the halt, and the blind;" and then, afterwards, "Go out into the highways," bring in the vagrants, the highway-men, "and into the hedges," bring in those that have no resting-place for their heads, and are lying under the hedges to rest, bring them in also, and "compel them to come in."

The poor. Yes, I see you this morning, you that are *poor.* I am to compel *you* to come in. You are poor in circumstances, but this is no barrier to the kingdom of heaven, for God hath not exempted from his grace the man that shivers in rags, and who is destitute of bread. In fact, if there be any distinction made, the distinction is on your side, and for your benefit—"Unto you is the word of salvation sent"; "For the poor have the gospel preached unto them." But especially I must speak to you who are *poor, spiritually.* You have no faith, you have no virtue, you have no good work, you have no grace, and what is poverty worse still, you have no hope. Ah, my Master has sent *you* a gracious invitation. Come and welcome to the marriage feast of his love. "Whosoever will, let him come and take of the waters of life freely." Come, I must lay hold upon you, though you be defiled with foulest filth, and though you have nought but rags upon your back, though your own righteousness has become as filthy clouts, yet must I lay hold upon you, and invite you first, and even compel you to come in.

The Maimed. And now I see you again. You are not only poor, but you are *maimed.* There was a time when you thought you could work out your own salvation without God's help, when you could perform good works, attend to ceremonies, and get to heaven by yourselves; but now you are maimed, the sword of the law has cut off your hands, and now you can work no longer; you say, with bitter sorrow—"The best performance of my hands dares not appear before thy throne." You have lost all power now to obey the law; you feel that when you would do good, evil is present with you. You are maimed; you have given up, as a forlorn hope, all attempt to save yourself, because you are maimed and your arms are gone. But you are worse off than that, for if you could not work your way to heaven, yet you could walk your way there along the road by faith; but you are maimed in the feet as well as in the hands; you feel that you cannot believe, that you cannot repent, that you cannot obey the stipulations of the gospel. You feel that you are utterly undone, powerless in every respect to do anything that can be pleasing to God. In fact, you are crying out—

> "Oh, could I but believe,
> Then all would easy be,
> I would, but cannot, Lord relieve
> My help must come from thee."

To you am I sent also. Before *you* am I to lift up the blood-stained banner of the cross, to you am

I to preach this gospel, "Whoso calleth upon the name of the Lord shall be saved"; and unto you am I to cry, "Whosoever will, let him come and take of the water of life freely."

The halt. There is yet another class. You are *halt*.

"Halt" is an old English word that means "lame."

You are halting between two opinions. You are sometimes seriously inclined, and at another time worldly gaiety calls you away. What little progress you do make in religion is but a limp. You have a little strength, but that is so little that you make but painful progress. Ah, limping brother, to you also is the word of this salvation sent. Though you halt between two opinions, the Master sends me to you with this message: "How long halt ye between two opinions? If God be God, serve him; if Baal be God, serve him." Consider thy ways; set thine house in order, for thou shalt die and not live. Because I will do this, prepare to meet thy God, O Israel! Halt no longer, but decide for God and his truth.

The blind. And yet I see another class—the blind. Yes, you that cannot see yourselves, that think yourselves good when you are full of evil, that put bitter for sweet and sweet for bitter, darkness for light and light for darkness; to you am I sent. You, blind souls that cannot see your lost estate, that do not believe that sin is so exceedingly sinful as it is, and who will not be persuaded to think that God is a just and righteous God, to you am I sent. To you too that cannot see the Saviour, that see no beauty in him that you should desire him; who see no excellence in virtue, no glories in religion, no happiness in serving God, no delight in being his children; to you, also, am I sent. Ay, to whom am I not sent if I take my text?

For it goes further than this—it not only gives a particular description, so that each individual case may be met, but afterwards it makes a general sweep, and says, "Go into the highways and hedges." Here we bring in all ranks and conditions of men—my lord upon his horse in the highway, and the woman trudging about her business, the thief waylaying the traveller—all these are in the highway, and they are all to be compelled to come in, and there away in the hedges there lie some poor souls whose refuges of lies are swept away, and who are seeking not to find some little shelter for their weary heads, to you, also, are we sent this morning. This is the universal command—compel them to come in.

Now, I pause after having described the character, I pause to look at the herculean labour that lies before me. Well did Melanchthon say, "Old Adam was too strong for young Melanchthon." As well might a little child seek to compel a Samson, as I seek to lead a sinner to the cross of Christ. And yet my Master sends me about the errand. Lo, I see the great mountain before me of human depravity and stolid indifference, but by faith I cry, "Who art thou, O great mountain? before Zerubbabel thou shalt become a plain." Does my Master say, compel them to come in? Then, though the sinner be like Samson and I a child, I shall lead him with a thread. If God saith *do* it, if I attempt it in faith *it shall be done;* and if with a groaning, struggling, and weeping heart, I so seek this day to compel sinners to come to Christ, the sweet compulsions of the Holy Spirit shall go with every word, and some indeed shall be compelled to come in.

Eight Appeals
My errand. And now to the work—directly to the work. Unconverted, unreconciled, unregenerate

men and women, I am to COMPEL YOU TO COME IN. Permit me first of all to accost you in the highways of sin and tell you over again my errand. The King of heaven this morning sends a gracious invitation to you. He says, "As I live, saith the Lord, I have no pleasure in the death of him that dieth, but had rather that he should turn unto me and live." "Come now, and let us reason together, saith the Lord, though your sins be as scarlet they shall be as wool; though they be red like crimson they shall be whiter than snow." Dear brother, it makes my heart rejoice to think that I should have such good news to tell you, and yet I confess my soul is heavy because I see you do not think it good news, but turn away from it, and do not give it due regard. Permit me to tell you what the King has done for you. He knew your guilt, he foresaw that you would ruin yourself. He knew that his justice would demand your blood, and in order that this difficulty might be escaped, that his justice might have its full due, and that you might yet be saved, *Jesus Christ hath died.* Will you just for a moment glance at this picture. You see that man there on his knees in the garden of Gethsemane, sweating drops of blood. You see this next: you see that miserable sufferer tied to a pillar and lashed with terrible scourges, till the shoulder bones are seen like white islands in the midst of a sea of blood. Again you see this third picture; it is the same man hanging on the cross with hands extended, and with feet nailed fast, dying, groaning, bleeding; me thought the picture spoke and said, "It is finished." Now all this hath Jesus Christ of Nazareth done, in order that God might consistently with his justice pardon sin; and the message to you this morning is this—"Believe on the Lord Jesus Christ and thou shalt be saved." That is, trust him,

Graphic descriptions such as this were virtually unheard of in early Victorian times. In an age when the curved legs of grand pianos were draped with cloth lest the young Prince of Wales be tempted to lust—in an age so sensitive as this, Spurgeon shocked many by the plainness of his speech.

renounce thy works, and thy ways, and set thine heart alone on this man, who gave himself for sinners.

I earnestly appeal to you. Well brother, I have told you the message, what sayest thou unto it? Do you turn away? You tell me it is nothing to you; you cannot listen to it; that you will hear me by-and-by; but you will go your way this day and attend to your farm and merchandize. Stop brother, I was not told merely to tell you and then go about my business. No; I am told to compel you to come in; and permit me to observe to you before I further go, that there is one thing I can say—and to which God is my witness this morning, that I am in earnest with you in my desire that you should comply with this command of God. You may despise your own salvation, but I do not despise it; you may go away and forget what you shall hear, but you will please to remember that the things I now say cost me many a groan ere I came here to utter them. My inmost soul is speaking out to you, my poor brother, when I beseech you by him that liveth and was dead, and is alive for evermore, consider my master's message which he bids me now address to you.

I command you. But do you spurn it? Do you still refuse it? Then I must change my tone a minute. I will not merely tell you the message, and invite you as I do with all earnestness, and sincere affection—I will go further. Sinner, in God's name I *command* you to repent and believe. Do you

ask me whence my authority? I am an ambassador of heaven. My credentials, some of them secret, and in my own heart; and others of them open before you this day in the seals of my ministry, sitting and standing in this hall, where

"Earnest"—a word Spurgeon uses six times in the sermon, and an attitude that is rife throughout. Most agree it was Spurgeon's sincere earnestness that made his preaching so effective.
Here, his first tactic is to plead with sinners as a friend.

God has given me many souls for my hire. As God the everlasting one hath given me a commission to preach his gospel, I command you to believe in the Lord Jesus Christ; not on my own authority, but on the authority of him who said, "Go ye into all the world and preach the gospel to every creature"; and then annexed this solemn sanction, "He that believeth and is baptized shall be saved, but he that believeth not shall be damned." Reject my message, and remember "He that despised Moses's law, died without mercy under two or three witnesses: of how much sorer punishment, suppose ye, shall he be thought worthy, who hath trodden under foot the Son of God." An ambassador is not to stand below the man with whom he deals, for we stand higher. If the minister chooses to take his proper rank, girded with the omnipotence of God, and anointed with his holy unction, he is to command men, and speak with all authority compelling them to come in: "command, exhort, rebuke with all long-suffering."

"We are ambassadors for Christ, as though God were entreating through us; we beg you on behalf of Christ, be reconciled to God" (2 Cor. 5:20, NASB).

I exhort you with my own testimony. But do you turn away and say you will not be commanded? Then again will I change my note. If that avails not, all other means shall be tried. My brother, I come to you simple of speech, and I *exhort* you to flee to Christ. O my brother, dost thou know what a loving Christ he is? Let me tell thee from my own soul what I know of him. I, too, once despised him. He knocked at the door of my heart and I refused to open it. He came to me, times without number, morning by morning, and night by night; he checked me in my conscience and spoke to me by his Spirit, and when, at last, the thunders of the law prevailed in my conscience, I thought that Christ was cruel and unkind. O I can never forgive myself that I should have thought so ill of him. But what a loving reception did I have when I went to him. I thought he would smite me, but his hand was not clenched in anger but opened wide in mercy. I thought full sure that his eyes would dart lightning-flashes of wrath upon me; but, instead thereof, they were full of tears. He fell upon my neck and kissed me; he took off my rags and did clothe me with his righteousness, and caused my soul to sing aloud for joy; while in the house of my heart and in the house of his church there was music and dancing, because his son that he had lost was found, and he that was dead was made alive. I exhort you, then, to look to Jesus Christ and to be lightened. Sinner, you will never regret—I will be bondsman for my Master that you will never regret it—you will have no sigh to go back to your state of condemnation; you shall go out of Egypt and shall go into the promised land and shall find it flowing with milk and honey. The trials of Christian life you shall find heavy, but you will find grace will make them light. And as for the joys and delights of being a child of God, if I lie this day you shall charge me with it in days to come. If you will taste and see that the Lord is good, I am not afraid but that you shall find that he is not only good, but better than human lips ever can describe.

The progression of Spurgeon's own conversion experience is so well stated in John Newton's famous poem,
"'Tis grace that taught my heart to fear,
And grace my fears relieved."

I reason with you. I know not what arguments to use with you. I appeal to your own self-interests. Oh my poor friend, would it not be better for you to be reconciled to the God of heaven, than to be his enemy? What are you getting by opposing God? Are you the happier for being his enemy? Answer, pleasure-seeker; hast thou found delights in that cup? Answer me, self-righteous man: hast thou found rest for the sole of thy foot in all thy works? Oh thou that goest about to establish thine own righteousness, I charge thee let conscience speak. Hast thou found it to be a happy path? Ah, my friend, "Wherefore dost thou spend thy money for that which is not bread, and thy labour for that which satisfieth not; hearken diligently unto me, and eat ye that which is good, and let your soul delight itself in fatness." I exhort you by everything that is sacred and solemn, everything that is important and eternal, flee for your lives, look not behind you, stay not in all the plain, stay not until you have proved, and found an interest in the blood of Jesus Christ, that blood which cleanseth us from all sin. Are you still cold and indifferent? Will not the blind man permit me to lead him to the feast? Will not my maimed brother put his hand upon my shoulder and permit me to assist him to the banquet? Will not the poor man allow me to walk side-by-side with him? Must I use some stronger words. Must I use some other compulsion to compel you to come in? Sinners, this one thing I am resolved upon this morning, if you be not saved ye shall be without excuse. Ye, from the grey-headed down to the tender age of childhood, if ye this day lay not hold on Christ, your blood shall be on your own head. If there be power in man to bring his fellow (as there is when man is helped by the Holy Spirit), that power shall be exercised this morning, God helping me. Come, I am not to be put off by your rebuffs; if my exhortation fails, I must come to something else.

I entreat you. My brother, I *entreat* you, I entreat you stop and consider. Do you know what it is you are rejecting this morning? You are rejecting Christ, your only Saviour. "Other foundation

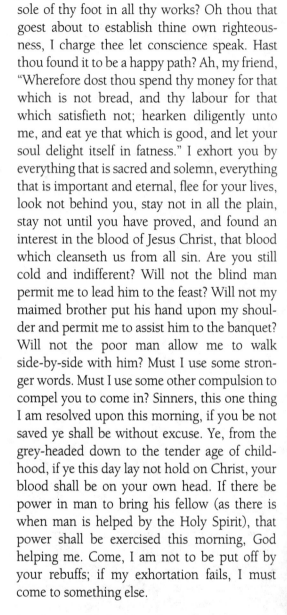

"When I say to the wicked, 'You shall surely die' and you do not warn him or speak out to warn the wicked from his wicked way that he may live, that wicked man shall die in his iniquity, but his blood I will require at your hand" (Ezek. 3:18, NASB).

can no man lay"; "there is none other name given among men whereby we must be saved." My brother, I cannot bear that ye should do this, for I remember what you are forgetting: the day is coming when you will want a Saviour. It is not long ere weary months shall have ended, and your strength begin to decline; your pulse shall fail you, your strength shall depart, and you and the grim monster—death, must face each other. What will you do in the swellings of Jordan without a Saviour? Deathbeds are stony things without the Lord Jesus Christ. It is an awful thing to die anyhow; he that hath the best hope, and the most triumphant faith, finds that death is not a thing to laugh at. It is a terrible thing to pass from the seen to the unseen, from the mortal to the immortal, from time to eternity, and you will find it hard to go through the iron gates of death without the sweet wings of angels to conduct you to the portals of the skies. It will be a hard thing to die without Christ. I cannot help thinking of you.

I see you acting the suicide this morning, and I picture myself standing at your bedside and hearing your cries, and knowing that you are dying without hope. I cannot bear that. I think I am standing by your coffin now, and looking into your clay-cold face, and saying, "This man despised Christ and neglected the great salvation." I think what bitter tears I shall weep then, if I think that I have been unfaithful to you, and how those eyes fast closed in death, shall seem to chide me and say, "Minister, I attended the music hall, but you were not in earnest with me; you amused me, you preached to me, but you did not plead with me. You did not know what Paul meant when he said, 'As though God did beseech you by us we pray you in Christ's stead,

"Death-beds are stony things without the Lord Jesus Christ."

Spurgeon entreats the lost with impassioned pleas. He vividly reminds them of the awful reality of death, hell, and judgment. Our calloused generation might cynically resist these entreaties, but not the Victorian. Their literature is replete with deathbed scenes. Recall the terror Jacob Morley feels in Dicken's *A Christmas Carol* as the Ghost of Christmas Yet to Come points to a snowy tombstone.

be ye reconciled to God.'" I entreat you let this message enter your heart for another reason.

I picture myself standing at the bar of God. As the Lord liveth, the day of judgment is coming. You believe that? You are not an infidel; your conscience would not permit you to doubt the Scripture. Perhaps you may have pretended to do so, but you cannot. You feel there must be a day when God shall judge the world in righteousness. I see you standing in the midst of that throng, and the eye of God is fixed on you. It seems to you that he is not looking anywhere else, but only upon you, and he summons you before him; and he reads your sins, and he cries, "Depart ye cursed into everlasting fire in hell!" My hearer, I cannot bear to think of you in that position; it seems as if every hair on my head must stand on end to think of any hearer of mine being damned. Will you picture yourselves in that position? The word has gone forth, "Depart, ye cursed." Do you see the pit as it opens to swallow you up? Do you listen to the shrieks and the yells of those who have preceded you to that eternal lake of torment?

Instead of picturing the scene, I turn to you with the words of the inspired prophet, and I say, "Who among us shall dwell with the devouring fire? Who among us shall dwell with everlasting burnings?" Oh! my brother, I cannot let you put away religion thus; no, I think of what is to come after death. I should be destitute of all humanity if I should see a person about to poison himself, and did not dash away the cup; or if I saw another about to plunge from London Bridge, if I did not assist in preventing him from doing so; and I should be worse than a fiend if I did not now, with all love, and kindness, and earnestness, beseech you to "lay hold on eternal life," "to

Is there a similarity here between Spurgeon and Jonathan Edward's classic sermon "Sinners in the Hands of an Angry God?"

labour not for the meat that perisheth, but for the meat that endureth unto everlasting life."

Some hyper-Calvinist would tell me I am wrong in so doing. I cannot help it. I must do it. As I must stand before my Judge at last, I feel that I shall not make full proof of my ministry unless I entreat with many tears that ye would be saved, that ye would look unto Jesus Christ and receive his glorious salvation. But does not this avail? Are all our entreaties lost upon you; do you turn a deaf ear? Then again I change my note. Sinner, I have pleaded with you as a man pleadeth with his friend, and were it for my *own* life I could not speak more earnestly this morning than I do speak concerning *yours*. I did feel earnest about my own soul, but not a whit more than I do about the souls of my congregation this morning; and therefore, if ye put away these entreaties I have something else—I must *threaten* you.

I threaten you. You shall not always have such warnings as these. A day is coming, when hushed shall be the voice of every gospel minister, at least for you; for your ear shall be cold in death. It shall not be any more threatening; it shall be the fulfillment of the threatening. There shall be no promise, no proclamations of pardon and of mercy; no peace-speaking blood, but you shall be in the land where the Sabbath is all swallowed up in everlasting nights of misery, and where the preachings of the gospel are forbidden because they would be unavailing. I charge you then, listen to this voice that now addresses your conscience; for if not, God shall speak to you in his wrath, and say unto you in his hot displeasure, "I called and ye refused; I stretched out my hand and no man regarded; therefore will I mock at your calamity; I will

He threatens the unbelievers with the truth of God's coming wrath. Life is frail, death is real. The apostle Paul wrote, "Knowing the terror of God, we can persuade men" (2 Cor. 5:11).

laugh when your fear cometh." Sinner, I threaten you again. Remember, it is but a short time you may have to hear these warnings. You imagine that your life will be long, but do you know how short it is? Have you ever tried to think how frail you are? Did you ever see a body when it has been cut in pieces by the anatomist? Did you ever see such a marvelous thing as the human frame?

> "Strange, a harp of a thousand strings,
> Should keep in tune so long."

Let but one of those cords be twisted, let but a mouthful of food go in the wrong direction, and you may die. The slightest chance, as we have it, may send you swift to death, when God wills it. Strong men have been killed by the smallest and slightest accident, and so may you. In the chapel, in the house of God, men have dropped down dead. How often do we hear of men falling in our streets—rolling out of time into eternity, by some sudden stroke. And are you sure that heart of yours is quite sound? Is the blood circulating with all accuracy? Are you quite sure of that? And if it be so, how long shall it be? O, perhaps there are some of you here that shall never see Christmas day; it may be the mandate has gone forth already, "Set thine house in order, for thou shalt die and not live." Out of this vast congregation, I might with accuracy tell how many will be dead in a year; but certain it is that the whole of us shall never meet together again in any one assembly. Some out of this vast crowd, perhaps some two or three, shall depart ere the new year shall be ushered in. I remind you, then, my brother, that either the gate of salvation may be shut, or else you may be out of the place where the gate of mercy stands. Come, then, let the threatening have power with you. I do not threaten because I would alarm without cause, but in hopes that a brother's threatening may drive you to the place where God hath prepared the feast of the gospel. And now, *must I turn hopelessly away?* Have I exhausted all that I can say? No, I will come to you again.

I answer your excuses. Tell me what it is, my brother, that keeps you from Christ. I hear one say, "Oh, sir, it is because I feel myself too guilty." That cannot be, my friend, that cannot be. "But, sir, I am the chief of sinners." Friend, you are not. The chief of sinners died and went to heaven many years ago; his name was Saul of Tarsus, afterwards called Paul the apostle. He was the chief of sinners, I know he spoke the truth. "No," but you say still, "I am too vile." You cannot be viler than the *chief* of sinners. You must, at least, be second worst. Even supposing you are the worst now alive, you are second worst, for he was chief. But suppose you are the worst, is not that the very reason why you should come to Christ? The worse a man is, the more reason he should go to the hospital or physician. The more poor you are, the more reason you should accept the charity of another. Now, Christ does not want any merits of yours. He gives freely. The worse you are, the more welcome you are. But let me ask you a question: Do you think you will ever get better by stopping away from Christ? If so, you know very little as yet of the way of salvation at all. No, sir, the longer you stay, the worse you will grow; your hope will grow weaker, your despair will become stronger; the nail with which Satan has fastened you down will be more firmly clenched, and you will be less hopeful than ever.

Look at the excuses Spurgeon answered. Are they still offered today? What other excuses do you hear? How can they be answered?

Come, I beseech you, recollect there is nothing to be gained by delay, but by delay everything may be lost. "But," cries another, "I feel I cannot believe." No, my friend, and you never will believe if you look first at your believing. Remember, I am not come to invite you to faith, but am come to invite you to Christ. But you say, "What is the difference?" Why, just this, if you first of all say, "I want to believe a thing," you never do it. But your first inquiry must be, "What is this thing that I am to believe?" Then will faith come as the consequence of that search. Our first business has not to do with faith, but with Christ.

Come, I beseech you, on Calvary's mount, and see the cross. Behold the Son of God, he who made the heavens and the earth, dying for your sins. Look to him, is there not power in him to save? Look at his face so full of pity. Is there not love in his heart to prove him *willing* to save? Sure sinner, the sight of Christ will help thee to believe. Do not believe first, and then go to Christ, or else thy faith will be a worthless thing; go to Christ without any faith, and cast thyself upon him, sink or swim. But I hear another cry, "Oh sir, you do not know how often I have been invited, how long I have rejected the Lord." I do not know, and I do not want to know; all I know is that my Master has sent me, to compel you to come in; so come along with you now. You may have rejected a thousand invitations; don't make this the thousandth-and-one. You have been up to the house of God, and you have only been gospel hardened. But do I not see a tear in your eye; come, my brother, don't be hardened by this morning's sermon.

O, Spirit of the living God, come and melt this heart for it has never been melted, and compel him to come in! I cannot let you go on such idle excuses as that; if you have lived so many years slighting Christ, there are so many reasons why now you should not slight him. But did I hear you whisper that this was not a convenient time? Then what must I say to you? When will that convenient time come? Shall it come when you are in hell? Will that time be convenient? Shall it come when you are on your dying bed, and the death throttle is in your throat—shall it come then? Or when the burning sweat is scalding your brow; and then again, when the cold clammy sweat is there, shall those be convenient times? When pains are racking you, and you are on the borders of the tomb? No, sir, this morning is the convenient time. May God make it so.

Remember, I have no authority to ask you to come to Christ tomorrow. The Master has given you no invitation to come to him next Tuesday. The invitation is, "*Today* if ye will hear his voice, harden not your hearts as in the provocation," for the Spirit saith "today." "Come *now* and let us reason together"; why should you put it off? It may be the last warning you shall ever have. Put it off, and you may never weep again in chapel. You may never have so earnest a discourse addressed to you. You may not be pleaded with as I would plead with you now. You may go away, and God may say, "He is given unto idols, let him alone." He shall throw the reins upon your neck; and then, mark—your course is sure, but it is sure damnation and swift destruction.

And now again, is it all in vain? Will you not now come to Christ? Then what more can I do?

I weep for you. I have but one more resort, and that shall be tried. I can be permitted to weep for you; I can be allowed to pray for you. You shall scorn the address if you like; you shall laugh at

Spurgeon weeps and prays for the lost in his congregation. It is said that thousands came to see Whitefield weep as well as to hear him preach. The tears of the earnest soul-winner are evident in the written account a century and a half old.

the preacher; you shall call him fanatic if you will; he will not chide you, he will bring no accusation against you to the great Judge. Your offense, so far as he is concerned, is forgiven before it is committed; but you will remember that the message that you are rejecting this morning is a message from one who loves you, and it is given to you also by the lips of one who loves you. You will recollect that you may play your soul away with the devil, that you may listlessly think it a matter of no importance; but there lives at least one who is in earnest about your soul, and one who before he came here wrestled with his God for strength to preach to you, and who when he has gone from this place will not forget his hearers of this morning. I say again, when words fail us we can give tears—for words and tears are the arms with which gospel ministers compel men to come in.

"... words and tears are the arms with which gospel ministers compel men to come in."

You do not know, and I suppose could not believe, how anxious a man whom God has called to the ministry feels about his congregation, and especially about some of them. I heard but the other day of a young man who attended here a long time, and his father's hope was that he would be brought to Christ. He became acquainted, however, with an infidel; and now he neglects his business, and lives in a daily course of sin. I saw his father's poor wan face; I did not ask him to tell me the story himself, for I felt it was raking up a trouble and opening a sore; I fear, sometimes, that good man's gray hairs may be brought with sorrow to the grave. Young men, you do not pray for yourselves, but your mothers wrestle for you. You will not think of your own souls, but your fathers' anxiety is exercised for you. I have been at prayer meetings, when I have heard children of God pray there, and they could not have prayed with more earnestness and more intensity of anguish if they had been each of them seeking their own soul's salvation. And is it not strange that we should be ready to move heaven and earth for your salvation, and that still you should have no thought for *yourselves*, no regard to eternal things?

Now I turn for one moment to some here. There are some of you here members of Christian churches, who make a profession of religion, but unless I be mistaken in you—and I shall be happy if I am—your profession is a lie. You do not live up to it, you dishonour it; you can live in the perpetual practice of absenting yourselves from God's house, if not in sins worse than that. Now I ask such of you who do not adorn the doctrine of God your Saviour, do you imagine that you can call me your pastor, and yet that my soul cannot tremble over you and in secret weep for you? Again, I say it may be but little concern to you how you defile the garments of your Christianity, but it is a great concern to God's hidden ones, who sigh and cry, and groan for the iniquities of the professors of Zion.

Now does anything else remain to the minister besides weeping and prayer? Yes, there is one thing else. God has given to his servants not the power of regeneration, but he has given them something akin to it. It is impossible for any man to regenerate his neighbor; and yet how are men born to God? Does not the apostle say of such an one that he was begotten by him in his bonds. Now the minister has a power given him of God, to be considered both the father and the mother of those born to God, for the apostle said he travailed in birth for souls till Christ was formed in them. What can we do then? We can now appeal to the Spirit. I know I have

"I cannot compel you, but thou O Spirit of God who hast the key of the heart, thou canst compel."

While the illustrations of this sermon are limited to similes, metaphors and allusions, Spurgeon's later messages contained far more anecdotes and historical and literary references.

preached the gospel, that I have preached it earnestly; I challenge my Master to honour his own promise. He has said it shall not return unto me void, and it shall not. It is in his hands, not mine. I cannot compel you, but thou O Spirit of God who hast the key of the heart, thou canst compel. Did you ever notice in that chapter of the Revelation, where it says, "Behold I stand at the door and knock," a few verses before, the same person is described, as he who hath the key of David? So that if knocking will not avail, he has the key and and will come in. Now if the knocking of an earnest minister prevail not with you this morning, there remains still that secret opening of the heart by the Spirit, so that you shall be compelled.

I thought it my duty to labour with you as though *I* must do it; now I throw it into my Master's hands. It cannot be his will that we should travail in birth, and yet not bring forth spiritual children. It is with *him;* he is master of the heart, and the day shall declare it, that some of you constrained by sovereign grace have become the willing captives of the all-conquering Jesus, and have bowed your hearts to him through the sermon of this morning.